# THE POTENTIALS OF OUR MEMORY

*How to train your memory to learn informations, names, books and school exams in a short time*

## VANESSA WILLIS

# Chapter One

# APPRECIATING THE HUMAN MEMORY CAPACITY

## Make up and Potentials of the Human Memory

No one will considerably achieve the aim and objective of a system or organization if there is no deep understanding and recognition of the potentials in that system. Without sounding like a broken record, it is acutely important to have a sit-down and appreciate all of the indices and factors as well as the benefits and demands of any project before we hit the start button. It is going to be to our hurt to be oblivious of the purpose and abilities of any system because we will trail the lanes of abuse and we can trust that the gratification or actualization we aim at will continue to be distant.

We must come to this acknowledgment that we have a limitless memory. Simple as that! Yet, it is kind of berserk because we do not appreciate the simplicity. Ironically, we would have to delve into complexities to help us appreciate the simple. The human memory is potentially the most unrivaled comprehensive and speedy information storage and processing system ever known to man. It is more of a case of being open to these potentials and appreciating them.

During a Fall Semester examination in a university, a Mathematics student went on a covert trip to a hill across a blue lake. The name wasn't documented – but really, that's not our business. Moving on, he went to a hill across a blue lake, his favorite location for his pity party. He did not need any allies around nor did he need to spend any cent on drinks or music- He had his tears for liquor and the crashing breeze of cold heaviness for the subtle theme. He was in peak frustration. He had been frustrated about his discipline – he had lost himself to failure and the only way he could muster some sense of sympathy and somber for his ground-breaking failures was to as well sit still and swing his head in heavy grief whilst piteous tears streamed down his cheeks. He was a sophomore year student who had nothing to himself other than his name and a lot of failing grades.

With his party in full swing, someone found him – not a student. As documented, the person was a musician who came to write a love song to his high school sweetheart – the song was about how the beauty of the blue lake could never stand the beauty of his sweetheart even if it tried. He was basically there to hurt nature with his melodies and symphonies by telling the blue lake boldly that its beauty is only a fraction of his sweetheart's beauty – how interesting.

So he found the troubled student who was already caught up in the gloominess of his one-man party and did a lot of convincing. As documented, it was said that the musician was actually very persuasive with his words. He was able to change the theme of a party he gatecrashed and left a momentous performance that was etched in the memory but not without taking his time to appreciate the reason for the dooms like an event.

"I must have a really slow memory... I can't comprehend anything...I can't remember anything." The student said with tears running down his face.

"That moment was profound. I felt his pain. I felt the energy behind the pain and somehow, it made me want to write a song for him, but unfortunately, writing a song for my sweetheart was more important. I hope he forgives me for that." The musician submitted while giving an account of how he helped a beaten student find a new lease of optimism and vigor for life.

This is not a storybook, so we are not going to go deep into the story. The point we are trying to bring out here is the student's utterance: "I must have a really slow memory...I can't comprehend anything...I can't remember anything."

Do you perhaps feel like this is the exact stage you are in; a stage where you find it rather difficult to remember or memorize the simplest things? Do you feel like your memory is slow? Do you feel like you cannot remember anything?

Follow through...

Know this, when people speak words like: "I have a bad memory", "my brain isn't that sharp", "I can't really store much information"; it is a negation to the facts that have been discovered about the human memory. According to research, the human memory has a capacity of about 1024 terabytes, which is equivalent to a petabyte or a million gigabytes. This means that human memory can store about 2.5 million gigabytes of information.

Apparently, there is no bad memory, there is no dull brain and there is no memory that cannot store that much information. Actually, 2.5 million gigabytes of information is nothing close to "my memory can't really store much information." So in a plot to decipher how the human memory works, how to use your memory effectively, how to learn new languages, how to prepare for your examinations and a couple of other perquisites that go along with your memory, it is essential to delete every negative voice that tells you that you cannot access all the potentials of your memory. Snuff out that voice that tells you the data is complex and your memory will not cope. You only need to shift your focus from your seeming inhibitions.

## THE POWER OF FOCUS

There are countless metaphors to fit the true meaning of focus into but it is imperative to harness what may seem to be downright unusual to link the power of focus with. In a plot to address this, the story of a seamstress from downtown Abbey, somewhere in London feels very profound to explain the power of focus. It's not a complex story at all; in fact, it perhaps shouldn't be called a story. She was asked a pretty simple question, and to everyone's surprise, she gave the most profound response anyone could ever give. In her words:

"I really do think the focus is relative...I mean, how you define it is relative. Having read over 200 articles on focus just out of curiosity, I don't think I have found anyone very sufficient. Okay, permit me to rephrase that – if I say I haven't found anyone very sufficient, that's me demeaning the perspectives of the writers – and I find that rather offensive. What I'm trying to say is that I haven't found any that tickles me so innately until I found one myself..."

The conversation took a dramatic turn when she gave everyone a plot twist, as though it was a fictional piece. Just as she earlier expressed – the focus is relative, focus indeed is relative.

What did she say?

She furthered:

"As I have already said, the focus is very relative. I

discovered the true meaning of focus in what seemed to be very mundane to me until it wasn't anymore – my ideology was radically changed. I have been a seamstress all my life – in fact, I can eloquently say that as a child, I could sew better than I could recite my nursery rhymes. Okay, that was a joke – perhaps a bad one…"

Everybody smiled.

She furthered:

"For over two decades now, I have had to put a sewing thread inside the sewing needle before I start sewing. I mean, that is the first thing I get to do daily before I start doing my job. Well, at times I don't do that. At times, I simply just sit and think about doing it – so in my head I'm still doing it without particularly doing it…"

Everybody smiled.

She furthered:

"For everyone who knows how minute a sewing needle is and how tiny the hole you have to insert the thread into is, you'd attest to the fact that it takes a lot of focus to do such. I remember a time I had a little problem with my eyes. I can't remember what the doctor called it again but it was basically just me seeing the opposite of everything. I'd look at a dog and see a lion. I'd look at a car and see a cockroach. I'd look at people and see zombies. At some point, I literally thought I was in Ellen Goldsmith Vein's Scorch Trials movie, but I wasn't. To cut my long story short, I later found a solution and it was pretty simple – all I had to do was wake up from my sleep. Apparently, I had been dreaming – so there was no doctor, no cockroach, and no zombies – thank the heavens.

Without further ado, I set out this day to do what I do daily, which is to simply pass the sewing thread into the sewing needle and I realized that I missed the hole a couple of times. It wasn't surprising – not at all because it happens that way every day. Sometimes, I don't miss it at all and sometimes I miss it a couple of times before getting a hold of the tiny hole. So for the sake of what we are talking about here, which is the focus, I want to particularly stress my perspective of what it means.

In the simplest form, I'd say being focused is me missing the hole a couple of times but never lose my gaze because I know I'm definitely going to get it..."

So I asked myself a question – "why do I always keep trying even when I don't get it a few times?" Then I realized that it is the assurance that I will still get it no matter how long it takes. My focus basically springs from a place of optimism and assurance.

What exactly am I trying to say? What I'm trying to say is that – following the popular opinion that says that you have to be disciplined to focus, you have to just keep at it and a whole lot of opinions. Well, they are very credible opinions but relatively speaking, I think you need a foundation to build your focus on. To me, you really cannot attain full focus until you have a fact or an assurance that what you're focusing on can actually work.

I simply just keep at the thread and the needle because I know it's definitely going to work. Do you get me at all?"

Silence blew across the room as everyone paused to ruminate on what the seamstress said. Her opinion was unpopular but it made a lot of sense to everyone. No one ever thought anyone could draw perspective from something seemingly inconsequential. But in the actual sense, it made a lot of sense to think of focus this way. You don't focus on something just because you are supposed to focus on it, you focus on something because it tickles you and you have an assurance that your focus will give birth to something in the end.

The bone of contention here is this – "Your focus is only as powerful as the motivation behind it."

"Your focus is only as powerful as the motivation behind it."

We talk about the power of focus as though it is something abstract. We spin it around science – well, maybe there is a scientific narrative backing it up. But in its raw sense, the power of focus ultimately depends on you and why you are doing what you do.

Drawing an inference from the seamstress' perspective, we can tell that it is the power of her focus that enables her to get hold of the tiny needle hole after a couple of misses. In corroboration, we can submit that:

Power is a word that stands on its own in this sense.

Focus is a word that stands on its own in this sense.

Power is the motivation behind your focus. To cement this, the phrase: "The Power of Focus" confirms that the word "Power" is behind the word, "Focus". Can you see that?

There is something about having an outline, an idea, a rough sketch of what, where and how something is to be achieved. We wake up in the morning and have a rough idea of what the major requirement of the day is supposed to be; is it a school day? Have I got a quiz coming up? A student might have a couple of questions on his or her mind as regards the school work demands for the day just as a businessman would have his preoccupation as regards how to drive his business forward and make more profits. The major goal to be achieved per day drives any decent person to put in efforts geared towards actualizing that goal. If for example, you are looking to build a house, you need to, first of all, decide the kind of house that is going to be and you get all the details down on paper. The architectural designs and all of the documents needed to guide the workers to create the house you envision are put in place to coordinate focus.

Working with our memory as humans is a very absorbing process that requires a level of imbuement. The thing about life basically is that there is always a process for everything. If it is something sustainable, then there is surely a process keeping it going. It is not enough to have an idea or to feel or perceive something;

that is the ground floor of the memory building. There is a process of conceptualizing this feeling, idea or perception for the memory to reproduce a decent representation of these items when required. The bottom line is this is a process. Yet, we will not be able to kick start this process without having a plan centered on a goal.

Focus connotes that we are paying attention to one particular thing at a time with the sole aim or goal of accomplishing or completing a particular task, without falling victim to distractions, total and absolute undivided attention. Definitely in the world, we live in right now, it is quite easy to get distracted on minor things, with the kind of things we are accessible to these days it is almost impossible to say you are totally focused on a particular thing and you won't leave it until you've achieved the goal to which you started in the very first place. The skill of paying attention is a very important factor in focusing. Unfortunately, it is a skill that a lot of people struggle with these days as a result of a myriad of activities that are tugging at our attention and wearing it thin. For students, they want to study and do well but at the same time, they want to play, have fun, go to parties and just enjoy life. For working-class people, they want to get a good job, make good money and at the same time go for parties and what have you. Focus requires full attention to a particular task at a time.

Going back to the inference drawn from the seamstress' perspective of focus - *Your focus is only as powerful as the motivation behind it*, we can establish the fact that you have motivation now – and the motivation is tied to the fact that your memory is a million times more sufficient than you think it is. Let your optimism be fueled by the assurance that you're not a dullard. You can take that language class. You can pass that tough examination. You can memorize things fast. And of course, you can store more information.

You might miss the needle hole a couple of times, but that doesn't mean you can't aim the hole the next time you try. There is only one way to get the thread into the hole – and it is by keeping at it. You just have to keep trying until you get it. The end is not vague, it is very visible – and the visibility is in the assurance that your memory can do far more than you think it can do.

What's the power behind your focus?

The power behind your focus is the profundity of your memory.

What is the profundity of your memory?

The profundity of your memory is the fact that your memory can store about 2.5 million of information.

With this being affirmed, you can begin to see things differently from now. You can begin to see potential where you see faults. You can begin to make moves where you've been reclining. And of course, you can begin inserting the sewing thread into the sewing needle again.

# Chapter Two

# AN ADVENTURE INTO WORLD OF THE MIND

Everyman at some points in their lives wants to feel on top of their world, recognized for achieving something important in the world around them at large. Either you want to be the first man who invents the teleportation machine or the time-traveling machine, which is still a theory until proven otherwise. Or maybe you are hoping to create something more valuable like a vaccine or cure to a deadly disease, or you just want to be as smart as Albert Einstein or William James Sidis who was quite possibly the smartest man to walk this earth as his IQ was estimated to be 50 to 100 points higher than Einstein's own. All these are achievable when you know the power and capability of your mind.

This book isn't aimed at explaining the biological and scientific formation of the brain but aimed at explaining and giving an insight of what the brain is capable of without having to complicate it with terms that might not be easily comprehensible. But it is of necessity to know the brain structure and have a basic understanding of how it works which will give you a better understanding of the brain. See it has learning to light a fire on the gas cooker before learning to cook a meal. Or to make it more cinematic, you can't watch Avenger Endgame and Infinity War without having watched the 18 previous installments that led to the ending of that saga, it's a necessary evil. This chapter will be the introductory part to a better understanding of the brain.

It needs no deep introduction in the role of the brain how and how important it is for it to be in perfect condition. A slight miscalculation or malfunction can disrupt some part of the body to function properly and cause an individual to be a patient in the Psych Ward. It is the central organ of the human nervous system and with the addition of the spinal cord, they make the nervous system.

Like every well-structured organization, the brain has its department and the role they play in helping humanity to be conscious of the world around them. To see, feel, express, understand; it's all the work of the brain. Humans will be useless without a brain. It's more or less like buying a computer without the Central Processing Unit or buying one that does not have a motherboard or a Hard-drive, its better off not bought at all.

The brain is divided into three major parts which are responsible for different functionalities.

We have the Forebrain, Midbrain, and Hindbrain. These major parts have different areas that have scientific names but would be broken down as easily as it can be. The names are; Occipital lobe, Temporal lobe, Parietal lobe, Frontal lobe, Cerebral cortex, Cerebellum, Hypothalamus, Thalamus, Pituitary gland, Pineal gland, Amygdala, Hippocampus, and the Mid-brain. If you are someone who quickly gets bored when you hear scientific names like these, I'd say we are in the same realm of thinking, but this chapter wouldn't be written if it doesn't have a role it will play in you reaching that position you want your brainpower. No one really wants to be like SpongeBob's Patrick who only has good ideas once in a blue moon.

We all want to be recognized for being intelligent, maybe you even want to be the smartest man alive, you might need to hold on a bit, sip the juice I forgot you to be telling you to place on your side table and read while the roles of these areas are being explained.

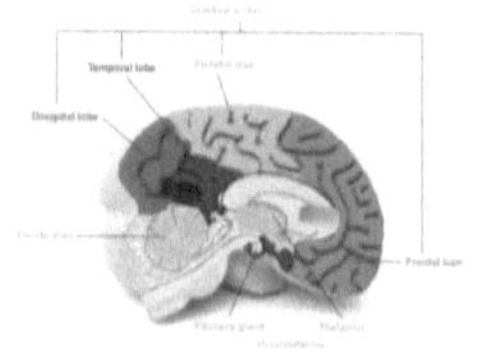

*O*ccipital Lobe: If you never forget objects or you're somewhat good at recognizing them whenever you sight the, then your Occipital lobe is in good condition. It's the part of the brain responsible for recognizing objects and also responsible for our vision. It is found at the back of the brain. This is found in the back of the brain

**Temporal Lobe**: These temporal lobes are found on either side of the brain and just above the ears. The temporal lobes are responsible for hearing, memory, meaning, and language which means they are in charge of learning and emotion.

**Parietal Lobe**: This can be found at the top back of the brain and responsible for the processing of impulses like touch, pain taste, temperature, etc. They also have language functions.

**Frontal Lobe:** It is concerned with emotions, reasoning, planning, movement, and parts of speech. It is also involved in purposeful acts such as creativity, judgment, and problem solving, and planning.

**Cerebral Cortex**: The cerebral cortex controls your thinking, voluntary movements, language, reasoning, and perception. This has a vital role to play in terms of the functionality of the brain.

**Cerebellum**: This controls movement, balance, posture, and coordination. And recently it has also been linked to thinking, novelty, and emotions.

**Hypothalamus**: controls your body temperature,

emotions, hunger, thirst, appetite, digestion, and sleep. Different areas of the brain compose **Hypothalamus and it's located at the base of the brain while it controls** very important behaviors.

**Thalamus:** controls your sensory integration and motor integration. Receives sensory information and relays it to the cerebral cortex. The cerebral cortex also sends information to the thalamus which then transmits this information to other parts of the brain and the brain stem.

**Pituitary gland**: This is the gland in charge of turning food to energy because without it you could eat a lot of food and still not get any energy from it and it also controls the body hormones.

**Pineal gland**: If you ever feel like you didn't grow as fast, probably you didn't get exposed to light because this gland start working after a baby is exposed to light. Without this gland working a baby will never grow. This gland is in charge of growth and maturity.

**Amygdala**: This comes in two categories and it's in control of the emotion, whether you're angry or mad. Without it, you could experience the best thing that can happen to a man and still not be happy about it.

**Hippocampus**: This is the one that forms and stores the memories without it nothing would be remembered by anyone. People with Alzheimer's disease lose the functioning of their hippocampus.

**Midbrain**: This section controls your breathing, reflexes, and the swallowing reflexes. It Includes the

Thalamus, Hippocampus, and Amygdala. Every living thing has to have a mid-brain.

**Medulla Oblongata**: This is responsible for maintaining vital body functions, such as breathing, digestion, and heartbeat. Difficulties in this area might not be a problem with the Medulla Oblongata as many diseases can hinder the proper functioning of the heart, digestive system, and breathing.

**Pons**: This part of the brain, control and sensory analysis. It vitally aids in consciousness and sleeping.

The above-listed parts of the brain have given a simplified function and roles the play to the adequate and proper functioning of the human body system. Inefficiency in the role the play has a high risk of being a problem with the brain rather than being a result of a disease or an infection. Whatever that affects the brain affects the body system as a whole.

The mind is very complex which it's full capabilities might never be unraveled till the end of times as different studies have shown different views on the functionalities and how exactly the mind works. The human mind can also be said to be in Triad. Three phases at which the brain works

The Conscious Mind, the subconscious, and the Unconscious are the three different realms at which the brain functions.

## CONSCIOUS MIND

This is best called being aware of something, the environment and being able to actively respond to the surroundings. During the conscious state of the mind, it can perform two basic functions which are being able to direct focus and also being able to imagine

While an important partner in the triad of the human mind, the conscious mind serves as a scanner for us. It will perceive an event, trigger a need to react, and then depending on the importance of the event, store it either in the unconscious or the subconscious area of the human mind where it remains available to us.

## SUBCONSCIOUS MIND

The subconscious mind is like a storage point for information that is being accessed frequently or recent memories such as people's names, skills needed to perform your daily job, etc.

## UNCONSCIOUS MIND

The unconscious mind is where all of our memories and past experiences reside. These are those memories that have been repressed through trauma and those that have simply been consciously forgotten and no longer important to us (automatic thoughts). It's from these memories and experiences that our beliefs, habits, and behaviors are formed.

There is a saying that goes you don't know what you're capable of till you try. Have you ever wondered how much information you can store in your memory? Probably you'd end up collapsing of having too much information in the head or might have to repress some memories of delete before you can store something else like computers do.

Before the dawn of technology, information was kept and passed along though writing on stones, and other archaic methods, and after technology, easier ways to keep information and making them accessible has come to the limelight and all of it has proven to be limited compared to the human mind. Even the greatest form of data storage namely the 5D superman memory crystal which can stockpile data up to 360 terabytes which is more than enough for one individual to use in a lifetime, but even this can't match up to the capability of the brain.

We all know the brain controls the information in the body with the help of the neurons which are billions in number. The brain command several functions (mood, language, skills, vision, memory, etc.) and its basic function are for it to encode and store information which eventually becomes memories that can be easily accessed way faster than you can type keywords in the computer to retrieve a piece of information. That's what makes the brain so special and it has been a mystery that has yet to be unraveled and frankly I think it might forever remain that way. The most amazing thing about the brain is that theirs is a calculated amount of the information that can be accumulated and stored which means the brain is unlimited. Unlimited space, the endless capability to store information and you don't have to buy more space or pay monthly to be able to have access to your information like the cloud saving which is a widely used way of storing information in the 21$^{st}$ century. And also "In raw data, our brains can compute 10 to the 13th and 10 to the 16th operations per second. This would be equal to more than one million times the people that there are on Earth. In essence and theory, the human brain is capable of solving and computing problems much quicker than a computer."

The brain is divided into two categories namely

1. Explicit (Declarative)
2. Implicit (Non-Declarative)

## EXPLICIT (DECLARATIVE)

Explicit or Declarative are the types of memories that can be expressed verbally. Like the name implies declarative. They are memories you can recall and pass across like dissemination of information. Examples are things, you were thought in class, that you still pass across to someone else probably while taking someone tutorial, or while trying to write it down in an examination. These types of memories are also known to be easily forgotten because of the disruption it creates while trying to form and stored information.

## IMPLICIT (NON-DECLARATIVE)

Implicit or non-declarative memories like the word implies are memories that can't be verbalized. These are memories that function on their own unconsciously. They ate mostly skills and they are the kind of memories the brain retains the most. An example is learning to knot a tie. It becomes easy once you know how to do it, but will be quite difficult to pass that kind of message along. This is a part of the brain that operates to make these kinds of information programmed that we don't have to be deep in thoughts to access that kind of information.

Of course how we retain information is totally different from one another, while some other people prefer reading, some people prefer hearing it and in some other cases, people don't remember what they don't experience. Information stored also has its duration. Information is stored for short term purposes while others are stored for long term usage.

## LONG TERM MEMORY

Long term memories are information stored for a long period, even though they deplete gradually, and sometimes it seems as though we have forgotten them they are still stored deep in our brains. The brain stores a lot of Long term memories and there's an indefinite amount to the amount of these kinds of information it can retain. There's still no actuality on whether we absolutely forget these kinds of memory or it becomes difficult to access.

## SHORT TERM MEMORY

Short term memories are stored to only serve for a very short period, seconds to minutes and these kinds of memories have limits to which they can be assimilated because the brain has to dump one before another short term memory can come in unless the information purposed to be short-lived is transferred to a long term memory and that can be done through the process called consolidation, better described and practicing or rehearsing the information in the short term memory.

The processes at which these information's are assimilated determine and decide if they would be short term memory or long term. Except you have a photographic memory and always remember everything you see when your brain won't function according to these theories or you have the shortest memory like that of

Clive Wearing who can only store information for 7 seconds then you have a lot of work to do.

To brief all this information as simple as it can be. The brain is like the sea and ocean, no matter the number of fishes and all kinds of aquatic animals in there, there would still be space for more. There is no definite number of how aquatic animals it can contain that would stop them from being able to move from one location to the other. Some sea creatures have a longer life span than the others. Or the brain can also be described as Space where our Planets and Nine other planets rotate and revolve around the sun. It's an infinite space that can contain trillions of planets and so is the brain.

The fact has been established that the mind is an unlimited space of information depending on one's intelligence and according to the creator of the World Memory Championship and inventor of Mind Mapping he said. "The human brain is like a muscle: exercise it and it gets stronger". The longer and frequently you work on your brain the better it gets at storing a countless number of information in the long term memory. Like the old saying goes Practice makes perfection.

# Chapter Three

# TRAINING THE MEMORY

Every other chapter you've read is everything you'll need before getting to this chapter, where you'll be thought ways at which you can train your mind. The fact has been established that the brain is also like the muscles the more you exercise it, the stronger it gets. We can't dispute the fact that some people are born genius and tend to acquire knowledge faster than we do. But some of these people aren't just born this way, the majority of them have a routine at which they read. Some of them are even slow learners by default but because they've spent time with themselves practicing and working their memory without people noticing which gradually increases the brainpower and makes them seem as if they were born that way. Learning to train your brain will definitely save you from a lot of problems, most especially if you're a student. You'll become a fast learner and the ability to recall more of what you've been thought or read and most importantly will save you from getting a brain disease (Alzheimer's wouldn't be a problem for you to deal with anytime in the future).

If you thoroughly follow the steps and tips in this chapter, you should be able to able to increase your brainpower to the level at which you want it to be. The only thing that you might not be able to achieve is having an Eidetic (Photographic) Memory. It's no news that photographic memory is the ability to recall an image, text or numbers from memory with high precision without using the mnemonic device (This is also known as a memory device. It's a learning technique that aids in information retrieval from the memory. This can be done by encoding, images or clues). Having a photographic memory will grant you the ability to recall memories like images, numbers, and text in great detail, most likely without missing anything. It is just like taking a mental picture of anything or better explains as photocopying a document. A few of these photographic memory events that have been reported to occur in a very small number of children and never in adults, but it has never been demonstrated to exist. Children possess this ability which is most likely going to be disrupted once the developmental changes set in, e.g. when they start to learn languages because acquiring language and verbal skills allows them to think more abstractly than using their visual memory. It has only been found in 2 to 10 % of children age 6 to 12.

This has only been perfectly demonstrated in movies Like Suits where Mike Ross a college dropout was able to get a job as a lawyer due to his photographic memory, and other movies. To be able to achieve this ability one would have to do with a lot of mental training, cognitive strategies and without mnemonic devices.

There are a lot of ways that you can amp up your brainpower and achieving the purpose at which you bought this book. The first step into memory training is;

## KNOW YOURSELF

The first step into achieving anything in life is knowing who you are and what you're capable of. Knowing your interest and capability is the very first step in achieving greatness and in this case, knowing your brain is very important. The level at which your brain is and how best you assimilate information is the very first step in training the memory.

Many had failed to increase their brain power by not studying themselves more. Different people have different ways of learning. Some people learn fast from things they read in books, on the internet, anything that comes in words for their visual satisfaction is what they grasp really fast. Some other people also learn faster from listening to people. There are few cases that an individual might read a book for a long period and won't really grasp anything from it until someone reads it to his or her ears. It's a case of preference and finding an easy way to increase brain power. Of course, you can always train yourself to be good to learn both cases but it's always easier if you start at the one you think you find easier, and if you don't know which it is you might need to start with one or try both to see which works better for you.

Studies have shown that our brain prefers images to text. In the process of the experiment, about 10% information that was passed orally was remembered by students after being tested 72 hours later but the number increased 65% after images were added to the learning process which proves that the brain retains memory faster when it comes in images, events that took place rather than oral or reading.

Of course, you might beg to differ probably because you still remember quite a lot of information that was passed to you orally. But if you would consider this; you'd realize when you watch a movie, or a soccer game or any event, there's a higher chance of you retelling the whole event without you missing anything. If perhaps the event was taped, if you come across it anywhere and you'll still remember where, when and everything that happened without having watched much from the tape, compared to you reading a whole textbook or a novel, and after a while, someone reads a line to you from the book you might not even tell which book it is until a piece of vital information is mentioned or a character from the book comes across in the reading before your brain picks it up. Nevertheless, reading is a necessity in the 21st century, but you have to discover what way you find it easy in acquiring knowledge otherwise the other tips might not make any difference. It shouldn't be something you must force, it has to be a gradual process; baby steps.

## WORK YOUR MEMORY

After discovering yourself and the way you best assimilate information, the next step is working your memory. Think of it as learning to drive a car, before the practical part start, you'd definitely use a couple of days to learn the theoretical aspect if not weeks before you take the driving test. After the long boring theoretical education of driving and you take the driving test which if you're lucky you passed on your first try. If after leaving driving school you don't drive a car for a very long time, you're pretty much the same with other people who haven't driven a car before, because the information you acquired was not put to use for a very long time. You practicalize or ruminate over it, the memory is as good as gone, and that's what working your memory is about. Any knowledge acquired that involves the whole operation of the brain is stays longer and is easily remembered than information that you acquire and you don't act on. It is the best way to work your brain and make you have a good memory is acting on it. That is, you should argue, think, practice and discuss it. The process at with it has required all the brain to work on the information gives it a higher chance of it sticking in your head as a long term memory.

## REPETITION

Have you ever wondered how you're able to sing word for word that is 7 minutes long and you can't even define chemistry without peeking into your textbook? One of the ways to improve brain capability is by doing that thing over and over again until it becomes stuck in your brain. To tell a short story, I remember back in college we were going to have a short test that morning and everyone knew the teacher preferred when we define or explain things the exact ways he did in class which made students paranoid over writing down everything he says during lectures. There was a particular definition we all knew would come out so everyone was cramming it because it was a very long one. I wasn't prepared because I missed his last lectures and no one remembered to tell me we were going to have a test. Everyone was preparing and trying to get as much as the can before they go in for the test. I don't really like reading, that's why I try as much as possible to attend every class, but it was unfortunate I didn't attend his last class because I assimilate faster when listening than when I read. There was this lady who kept reading aloud everything she had earlier; she kept saying it over and over till it got my attention. It was a very long defi-nition and some other topics; I decided not to read through my notes anymore as I listened to her as she kept ranting. Once she was done with the whole topic she'd start all over again. She kept reading over and over till I was able to grasp 50% of it without having to go through the stress of reading which will take me longer to assimilate. I have also vividly spoken about the neces-sity of knowing yourself, but since this is another segment I'm going to use the story to further explain the power of repetition.

The lady that kept repeating the topic was increasing her brainpower by practicing repetition. Even though she was most likely going to forget after a short period, because she was only reading to offload in from her head during the test, but there are chances that she might never forget if the information has moved to the long term memory. And also the repeti-tion hasn't only helped her but also helped me because I kept listening to it over and over again it has helped me memorize it too and trust me I still remember every word of it till today. That's the power of repetition, it's more like listening to a particular repeatedly, into the time you'd know the lyrics to the song and it'll forever be in your brain. This doesn't only apply to reading; it also applies every kind of knowledge acquired. Because doing it repeatedly, the brain automatically finds ways to make you do it easier and faster. The more you train your brain in with tips like this the easier it becomes for you to learn and retain knowledge for a long period. The fictional Angus MacGyver wouldn't be mentally healthy if he wasn't practicing a lot of life hacks that made him very good to the point of manipulation anything in his surroundings to his advantage.

## EXERCISE (WORKING THE BODY)

Of course, this book isn't meant to discuss anything on physical fitness but how to train your brain, but do you know when you exercise the body, it does not just improve your physical health but it also aids in the mental growth. When you exercise the body it helps you learn faster, makes you more alert as it helps the brain create neural connection faster which also mean the brain will process information faster. So if you're not the sporty kind of person or you feel it's not necessary, trust me it is. Exercising for at least 30 minutes in a day has a long way to go in increasing your brainpower. But if you're a regular exerciser, you've gone a very long way to achieving your dreams in this brain quest. And remember the more you're following these rules and tips you're making your brain better one step of the way and it can't get worse. You can be dumber by following these rules, even if you only follow one of these rules, it helps a long way, but to get a more vibrant result you will need to follow all the rules, the aforementioned and the ones that will follow.

## GETTING ENOUGH SLEEP

It is important that you get enough sleep. In a very high case, most poor memory performance has been associated with not sleeping regularly. One thing you might not know about sleep is that it doesn't only make the body rest, but the brain too. The only time the brain isn't fully resting when you're sleeping is when you have nightmares. It means some part of your brain is still working. Not getting enough sleep negatively affects the brain, and it doesn't help with memory consolidation, which is transferring short term memory to long-lasting memory. A couple of years back, a study was done on the effects of sleep in 40 children between the ages of 10 and 14. The children were divided into two groups. One group had training and memory tests in the evening and had another in the morning after having a goodnight's sleep, while the other group was tested twice on the same day with no sleeping interval. The group that slept performed 20% higher than the other group when a memory test was done.

Research shows adults should get seven to nine hours of sleep in a day, teenagers should get around eight to nine hours. Children age 7-12 years should get ten /to eleven hours of sleep. Children aged 3-6should get ten to 12 hours while toddlers should get 12 hours of sleep overnight for them to reach optimal health and brainpower.

If you are probably a very busy person and you don't

get enough sleep at night, your memory will be slowly depleting as your IQ will slowly reduce. You can't cheat nature, but if you've found a way to cheat nature and deprive yourself of sleep then you're slowly affecting your body. A night of good and full sleep is the one that you're absolutely unconscious to the world around you. If someone opens your door to your room as silent as possible and you heard? Then be rest assured that you are taking a full sleep; it can also be related to napping. Some of your senses are still fully fictional which means your brain is also working. If you're sleep deprived there's a high chance of your having time lapses, loss of memory or you won't be remembering stuff. You don't need to have a brain problem before that can happen to you.

I must confess, most times it very hard to keep a healthy sleeping cycle with all the hard work we have to put in our lives to making money daily or your favorite show start airing very late in the night. I understand how tempting that can be, but all these have to be sacrificed to help your brain. Even while writing this book I always have to stay up late at night to get some things written down, but also get affected. Terrible headaches and I'll also find it hard to fall asleep because I didn't get much sleep as I'm supposed to. Don't eat late at night and take sleep early preferably before 10 and you're up to have a quality brain and increased IQ.

## MEMORY TEST

We aren't in the Stone Age anymore, not even the Industrial Age. With the growth of technology and smartphone and with the help of brilliant people who have been able to come up with applications and software that we can use to test out the brain. Always take brain test or play brain quiz games. This will further improve your IQ and memory capability. These application and software have strategically been created to increase out reasoning and they wouldn't be created it f it does no good. There are quite a number of them that you can install on your laptops and cell phones, so do not hesitate to do so.

## DRINK LESS ALCOHOL

I'm a firm believer that alcohol does little to no good to the body system. Of course, if you search the internet it'll definitely have its advantage, but to the body system, I can't say it does much good most especially to the brain. Drinking too many alcoholic beverages is detrimental to your health and will do more harm than good most especially to the brain and memory. Even though alcohol doesn't make you forget anything when you drink to stupor and you black out the brain loses its ability to create any memory. I'm not saying you shouldn't take alcohol anymore if you don't want to take it anymore? Good for you, but if you can't do without it at least reduce the intake.

Binge drinking, that is, consuming large volumes of alcohol at a go is patterned to raise your blood alcohol level than usual and it alters the brain and results in memory deficit. If you're a student who practices binge drinking, wither weekly, daily or monthly. You'll find it harder to recall memories during tests compared to a student who doesn't binge drink. Repeated binge drinking can and will damage the hippocampus (This is the one that forms and stores the memories without it nothing would be remembered by anyone). Therefore avoid excessive intake.


## LEARN A NEW SKILL

Do you want to know why learning a new skill is important? I'll also tell this with a story. It wouldn't be a true story like the one I previously told. I'll be picking it from the movie this time around Suits (One of my favorite movies by the way) Rachael Zane was a paralegal in a law firm and she worked so hard every day and she was good at what she does, in fact, she was one of the best. But soon she got tired of being a paralegal and decided to chase her life-long dream of going to Harvard University to study law and to become a lawyer. That is when she realized she needed to learn a new skill, to help her career but of course, she's no medical practitioner but there's no way she'd know she was helping brain too. She was already frustrated with her job and learning a new skill would help her channel the frustration to help her in getting to a more prominent place in her career. The brain loves learning new things, and when you do that, it gradually gives you focus and something to aim for. I am going to personally start learning computer programming, not because I want to make the next-generation software, but because I need to feed my brain and feed it by giving it new information. And when learning becomes a habit, you'll find your ability to remember and recall things effortlessly, becomes a habit too.


## DRINK LOTS OF WATER

No amount is too small for your body; believe me, you will not drown. The specialists recommend we take 4-5 liters of water daily and since the brain is made up of 70% water you should know now that it wouldn't function at its best if you don't drink as much water as possible. Drinking enough water will give you the ability to concentrate, you'll be more decisive and you won't feel like the energy is being drained from your body for no reason. Of course, when you drink lots of water you'll need to visit the bathroom a couple more times than usual but that I tell you that is also a good thing. Therefore always stay hydrated to help your brain function properly.

## MEDITATION

This is one thing that every human being must practice. It's not just about closing your eyes and sitting in a lotus position. It is about freeing your brain from every thought and trying to calm your system.

Sometimes things get very tough and strenuous and you have a lot to do. You don't necessarily need to sleep before you can help the brain focus more. Most especially when an individual is frustrated, it seems impossible to get anything right, that because the brain is disoriented and you might be overloading it. Of course, the brain can process a lot of information at the same time without being overwhelmed. There's only so much the brain can do and absorb at the same time even if you think you're really good at multitasking, the brain can't absorb a tremendous amount of information at the same time. Like I said you don't necessarily need to sleep. All you need to do is calm yourself, you can take a walk; listen to cool music, just to give your mind more focus. 10 minutes is okay and you'll notice the difference and more efficiency in the function of the brain.

## EAT HEALTHIER

This part really had to come last because it's a lot on its own. There's really no point in trying to train your memory if you're not eating right. There's a saying that goes "You're what you eat". This means there's a part of you that can be defined or predicted based on the kind of things you swallow. To up the capability of your brain, these are some of the foods you need to start eating.

The kind of food you eat determines how efficiently your brain will perform. If you're the kind of person that eats lots of junks, you're not only harming your physical health but also your mental health.

One thing you should know is sugary foods even though the body needs sugar for energy, but when this gets too much in the body system, it affects the brain. Several food items help the brain. You might be surprised by some kind of food that will be listed. If you didn't know by now the brain is only 3% of your body weight but it uses up to 17 percent of your energy, therefore eat right for both the body and the brain.

If you want to have a healthy brain you'll have to eat healthily. Mind you the least will be long because I understand that you might be allergic to some listed food. There's no point in trying to eat food to increase your brainpower if you're going to die in the process.

## NUTS

Studies have shown that a high intake of Vitamin E which is abundant is Nuts (Walnuts, Almonds) it helps the brain grow. Some other nuts also contain amino acids which help in stress reduction. I understand that many people are allergic to nuts. You don't need to take this as other food items can also give you this kind of advantage.

## BLUEBERRIES

Blueberries have been discovered to have a high amount of antioxidant which is helpful for short term memory and correlation. Even though other berries are also beneficial to brain growth, blueberries have proven to be the best. So if you haven't been taking this, I think its high time you started.

## TOMATOES

I know you would be surprised if I told you tomatoes is highly advantageous to dementia patients. Dementia patients are known to have radical damage in the brain which tomatoes are one way to prevent that for people who don't have that kind of ailment. It protects the brain, I don't see any reason why you shouldn't take it.

## BROCCOLI

Broccoli is packed full of antioxidants, is well-known as a powerful cancer fighter and is also full of vitamin K, which is known to enhance cognitive function. Like it has been earlier pointed out that the brain uses 17% of body energy and that makes it vulnerable to free-radical damage and the antioxidants in Broccoli helps in terminating the threat

## FOODS RICH IN FATS

The brain is composed of 60% fat, to repair and synapses associated with the memory processes. The brain needs essential fatty acids as it is the fattest organ in the body system. The body does not naturally produce essential fatty acids so we must get them in our diet.

Food items that provide the essential fatty acids include eggs, flax, fish (salmon, sardines, mackerel, herring).

## SOY

Soy to the brain helps improve memory and mental flexibility because it is full of proteins that trigger the neurotransmitters associated with memory. Soy, along with many other whole foods mentioned here, is full of proteins that trigger neurotransmitters associated with memory.

## DARK CHOCOLATE

One amazing thing you should know is the darker your chocolate the more nutritious it is to the brain. If you're consuming up to 70% cocoa which chocolate is made of, its abundance in flavanol antioxidants will increase the blood flow to the brain and shield brain cells from aging.

## FOODS RICH IN VITAMINS: B VITAMINS, FOLIC ACID, IRON

The above-listed nutrients are not essential to human growth; they are particularly favorable to the brain. The list of available vitamins goes on and on but some Vitamin B prevents the high risk of stroke and cognitive impairments like Alzheimer's disease. Some great foods to obtain brain-boosting B vitamins, folic acid and iron are kale, chard, spinach and other dark leafy greens.

Other sources of B vitamins are liver, eggs, soybeans, lentils and green beans. Iron also helps accelerate brain function by carrying oxygen. If your brain doesn't get enough oxygen, it can slow down and people can experience difficulty concentrating, diminished intellect, and a shorter attention span. To get more iron in your diet, eat lean meats, beans, and iron-fortified cereals. Vitamin C helps in iron absorption, so don't forget the fruits!

## FOODS RICH IN ZINC

Food rich in zinc has also proven to be efficient in the increment in brain-building and thinking capability. The duty of Zinc is to stabilize and regulate the communication between neurons and the hippocampus. Zinc is deposited within nerve cells, with the highest concentrations found in the hippocampus, the part of the brain responsible for higher learning function and memory. Pumpkin seeds, liver, nuts, and peas, are food items that are known to be concentrated with Zinc.

## GINGKO BILOBA

This herb has been utilized for centuries in eastern culture and is best known for its memory-boosting brawn. It can increase blood flow in the brain by dilating vessels, increasing oxygen supply and removing free radicals.

## GREEN AND BLACK TEA

A lot has been said about green and black tea. Some say it calms the mind, some have claimed it makes an individual live longer. I'm not saying it can't do that, but I'm only going to point out the benefits it has to increase your brain. Acetylcholine is a chemical found in the brain that helps the memory. The work of this green and black tea is to breakdown this chemical which is lacking in people that an individual suffering from Alzheimer's disease.

## SAGE AND ROSEMARY

Talking of increased memory and clarity these herbs are highly recommended to help in performing that task. Try to enjoy these herbs in your favorite dishes.

However, you should know, nothing works overnight, don't expect results overnight: this may take a few weeks to build up in your system before you see improvements as long as you're persistent.

When it comes to mental magnitude, eating smart can really make you smarter.

Do you remember the last time you set a goal for yourself to hit the gym at least, three times a week so you could keep form and lose that weight you gained over time? If you remember clearly, the reason why you set this goal for yourself was so you could be in a better form and also train your muscles for better flexibility, right? Aside from this, you also know that exercise has been proven by physicians to be one of the best lifestyles to engage to live a healthy lifestyle.

People who survived an accident and have been static for a while are being advised to go through physiotherapy just to restore their stamina and composure. Indeed, as you already know, the importance and benefits of exercise cannot be completely contained due to its vastness.

So what's the point here?

The point is this – just as your body needs physical exercise to maintain a good shape and a good form, your brain also needs to be exercised so you can have a good memory that grasps and assimilate things really fast. Physicians will tell you that it's the muscle you exercise that gains strength and flexibility – if you don't exercise your muscles, they'd be redundant and relaxed.

Do you need a redundant muscle? No, you do not.

Do you need a relaxed muscle? Definitely not.

In this case, your muscle is your brain – you need to train your brain to attain the strength and flexibility you need. Just like the natural elastic theory, the more you pull, the more your elastic stretches – the same applies to your brain. The more you train your brain, the sharper it becomes.

A friend once said:

"I think it is an absolute mockery to think that you can exhaust the capacity of your brain. And it's totally absurd to think that your brain will shut down if you work it too much. No, the brain never shuts down and you just can never exhaust the capacity of your brain. No human has even used up to 20 percent of his/her brain capacity – so how do you get scared that your brain will shut down. The brain is not some computer hard drive and neither is it a cell phone operating system – the more you use it, the better it gets. So I think the greatest gift man was given by the universe is the brain – I mean, the only way we even know we have something called brain is because we have something called the brain. Isn't that just hilarious?

When I realized I could actually train my memory, everything changed for me. I started the training procedure and my memory kept getting better, sharper and friendlier. I can't say I fully understand what exactly transpired in my medulla oblongata, but I knew something had changed. Theories that were so complex for me before became the easiest things I could do.

I really do think everyone should engage in the memory training culture."

## HOW THEN DO I TRAIN MY MEMORY?

Here are the five most powerful ways to train your memory:

### Engage in physical exercises

You might be wondering what engaging in physical exercises have to do with your memory – well, you should be curious. Do you know that your brain controls all your bodily responses and it receives signals from every healthy activity you engage yourself in? Anytime you set out to carry out a physical exercise to put your body in better shape, the result isn't just beneficial to your bones and muscles alone – it is also beneficial to your brain because your brain is your body. If your brain is affected, your body cannot function properly. In fact, without the brain, you are just a vegetable. So engaging in physical exercises boosts your brain reception more than you think.

Don't stop engaging in exercises!

## Pick up an activity that's out of your league

Perhaps this is the most challenging part of memory training. Many people run away from this part of the process because they believe it stresses them out a lot. But really, does any good thing come easy? Picking up an activity that's out of your league isn't stressful at all; all it needs is your discipline. It gets easier when you attack from the understanding that it is all part of the process of training your memory.

When you pick up skills like learning the guitar, learning a new language, trying out something you've never tried before – it challenges your brain on a different level and stretches its elasticity. As you engage yourself in the new skill, it's going to feel strange and somewhat difficult to you, but it's not – it really does get easier as you do it consistently. The reason why it might feel difficult at first is that your brain starts by trying to acclimatize itself to the new challenge, and through this process, it improves and stretches till the new skill becomes second nature to you.

While doing this, you will definitely be tempted to give up, but just know that it gets easier as you try harder. It is not beyond you. Your memory is about to receive a boost.

## Get adequate sleep

Adequate sleep is perhaps the most underrated gift of life. Many people do say that they wish they never had to sleep – but how can we regain our strength when we don't sleep? Just the way your body gets weak after a tedious physical activity, your brain also gets weak to – and just like your body needs rest every time it gets stressed, your brain also needs rest so it can regain its strength. The only proven and known way the body regains strength is through proper rest – and this is why you'd see medical doctors advise their patients to sleep well even when their problem is not sleeping. The reason why they recommend sound sleep for every patient is that human sleep is designed to perform the function no medication can ever perform in the body system. In fact, without proper sleep, recommended medications cannot work.

When you get adequate sleep, it rejuvenates your brain and allows the stressed cells to regain their strengths so you can feel fresh when next you start the brain training procedure.

So how long should an adequate sleep last?

Adequate sleep should last for about 7 to 9 hours depending on the person. Any sleep within this time-frame can be tagged as adequate.

## Play intellectual games

Games like Sudoku, Lumosity, Happy Neuron, My Brain Trainer, Crosswords, Braingle, etc. are some intellectual games you can engage yourself with, perhaps during your leisure time. To train your memory, you need activities that challenge its usual path. In case you don't know. Your brain actually has a functioning path. For instance, if you have a daily habit of playing the guitar for at least an hour daily – as a result of this, your brain has a way of craving this even when you don't want to play it. Your brain naturally invites you to go pick your guitar up because that's the functioning path you have trained it to follow. This is one of the reasons why people who have addiction problems find it difficult to quit whatever they are addicted to. It is so because their brains have been wired to function a certain way.

So when you engage your brain in playing intellectual games that require you to do a lot of thinking to advance to the next level, your brain automatically begins to task your memory to act sharp at every given time – which then helps improve the power of your memory.

## Get creative

Have you ever sat to think of what creativity actually means? Creativity has to do with making things that seem complex or abstract really simple. Getting creative can help you train your memory a lot because it challenges your brain to function on the different wavelengths. When your brain gets creative, it searches through the scope of life to coin perspective from seemingly inconsequential concepts to meet the purpose you are tasking it for.

A writer once shared a few tips on how he gets creative with his writing.

He said:

"Creativity is very simple. I basically just pick a draft I had written and rewrite it in a totally different way without toning down its message or anything at all. While doing this, I discovered that my brain waves were no longer human – they became demons of creativity."

To get creative, you can try doing the regular things you do daily in a different way to achieve the same result. Think about it deeply – it's okay if it takes a lot of time, just keep thinking. Afterward, you'd be amazed at how getting creative can turn your brain into a demon of creativity.

# Chapter Four

# GETTING THE BEST OUT OF EVERY EXAMINATION

Henry Fischel's legacy set the pace for a system which just like others has its advantages and disadvantages. We can peg one of the major contributions of examinations at the fact that this invention has been the benchmark for all professional accreditations across the globe. Yet, a lot of critics will still readily posit that it is not exactly a true representation of a person's abilities. Whichever side of the divide on which you are, students generally would not bat an eyelid if it gets yanked. Most perhaps will give their pocket money to see it canceled if that is worth anything. There is no doubt that what qualifies anyone to mount another pedestal is the ability to prove the worthiness to be promoted through examinations. Educational institutions, financial institutions, sports academy, religious institutions, and you name it have made it a culture to test individuals through different modes of examination before they are granted particular access or giving a certain hierarchy. And come to think of it, the reason why you can read this piece of literature with so much ease is that it has passed through series of scrutiny and examination to certify its reading credibility for your sake. An examination is like air, you barely forge ahead in life without it. Know this, if you find a man who has succeeded without having passed through any form of examination, that man is not a man. He's probably an unknown entity in a man's body.

You don't have to be in the four walls of your school to participate in an examination; every waking day is n examination for you. Actually, you are faced with different choices every day and you are to pick the one that will benefit you. In this case, which do you pick? How do you know the right one to pick? How do you know the wrong one not to pick? You can see it's more like a conflict going on in your head and if you are not well equipped to make the right choices, you just might be deeply affected negatively.

Don't get this twisted, this is an introduction. The bone of contention here is how you can equip yourself to get the best out of every exam. Do you remember the story of the university student who was lamentably melancholic as a result of his incessant failure? Right, you do. Now, should his story be a metaphor for everything you are going through right now with your exams or not? Do you feel frustrated about the outcomes of your school grades and really wish a change could arise from somewhere or perhaps someone comes in to help you?

Here is the deal; the change and the victory you require over your examination are all in your hands, and it has to do with how well you learn to put your awesome memory to test. It has already been established that human memory is in nowhere close to insufficient when it comes to storing information. And to be very factual, the human brain is actually unlimited. So for you to be struggling with your memory is a validation that you've not learned how to properly utilize and maximize the strength of your memory.

Effectively utilizing and maximizing your memory has to do with proper organization of information in your memory. So frankly, a good memory is a memory that can organize information appropriately. In respect to this, there is a need to stress what you already know as a student, and as well as a human being – and it is the fact that some things come before some things. What is the point here? The point is that to be able to organize information appropriately in your memory, you have to first master the art of organizing yourself.

"To be able to organize information appropriately in your memory, you have to first master the art of organizing yourself."

An unorganized self cannot properly organize information in the brain. As you can see, everything starts with you. Self-organization has perhaps proven to be one of the most difficult aspects of man's life because every human is actually born with a profound impulsive tendency that makes you want to do things however they come without particularly having a structured plan. To date, many are paying thousands of dollars to have professionals teach them how to manage themselves properly. And if you want to be frank with yourself, you'd realize that proper self-management is not an inborn gift, it is an acquired skill that takes profuse intentionality from you. And if you can give this skill what it wants, which is your wholehearted discipline, you can be sure to have things go more smoothly than they would usually go.

Take a moment and think deeply. Ruminate over how organized your life is as a person. Can you confidently say your life is organized? Or better still, honestly answer the following questions:

Since our main focus right now is getting the best out of every examination, the questions are going to be streamlined a bit.

- Do you have proper time management as a student?
- When do you start preparing for your examinations?
- Do you consider yourself a fast reader or a slow reader?
- Do you have power behind your focus?
- Do you know your time?

If you think deeply, you'd realize that these questions are life-defining questions every student should be able to answer with all honesty. The answers to these questions can undoubtedly determine how best you make of your memory.

Let's take them one after the other...

## DO YOU HAVE PROPER TIME MANAGEMENT AS A STUDENT?

Whether smart or dull; whether fast or slow; whether male or female; whether rich or poor – everyone has the same amount of time daily, which is 24 hours. And unfortunately, there is nothing no man can do to increase or decrease it – it is everlasting and there is no questioning it. When we talk about time management, we are talking about how you manage your 24 hours as a student. Do you spend more or less time studying?

Okay, let's clear this – this is no moral code literature that gives you cautionary tales on how to be serious with your studies and all that – no, that is not the purpose of this literature. The purpose of this is to validate and expose the fact that your memory is actually enough for you to excel and do all the things you require it for. It is also to let you know that you cannot possibly exhaust the capacity of your memory.

Moving on, there is a need to properly organize your time to be able to organize information in your memory. According to various researches, it has been confirmed that the human brain functions with time. To further expand this fact in the practical sense, have you ever wondered why your brain automatically knows nighttime is for sleep, while daytime is for functioning? Believe it or not, your brain understands your body more than you do; and so does your memory understands time more than you do. This is why some people would tell you that they are nocturnal. What this means is that they are in their full functionality at nighttime – and this is not for everybody. Some people cannot do anything at night rather than sleep – and it is definitely not a bad thing, it's just a product of their body functions.

Speaking of proper time management, it is not the same as mastering the time of the day and what every time should seem like – it is basically having productive experiences with your 24 hours. Know this, the difference between excellence and mediocrity is the productivity of time.

"The difference between excellence and mediocrity is the productivity of time."

You probably didn't see that coming, but that is what it is. The reason why some people are excellent at what they do and some people are mediocre at what they do is because the excellent people understand that the more the productivity, the closer they get to excellence – and on the other hand, the ones whose standards are mediocre have little or no reverence to time.

In a nutshell, proper time management has to do with how productive your 24 hours is.

Now, think about it, do you have proper time management?

## WHEN DO YOU START PREPARING FOR YOUR EXAMINATIONS?

"When you start determines how well you pass"

This isn't merely an examination tip; it is a tip on how to handle and prepare for situations that cut across all walks of life. So believe this – when you start determines how well you pass. Try imagining having to catch up a 7 am flight from Washington to Arkansas and you only start packing your bags at 6.45 am that same morning when you'd still have to take a forty-two minutes' drive to the airport. There is no doubt about it; you are definitely going to miss that flight.

This still balls down to time management and productivity. You should know the right time for everything to achieve the best result. Everything is not the function of your memory; it is also about making the right choices for yourself.

Now, think about this – when do you start preparing for your examinations? Do you start early enough or rather late?

## DO YOU CONSIDER YOURSELF A FAST READER OR A SLOW READER?

Veronica Baines and Jeremy Knowles ran an experiment to test how fast they'd assimilate a page of certain Chemistry textbook to test how fast they'd assimilate the content of the page. They agreed to read through the page and assimilate for an hour. They both did and after an hour, came together to give a report. Veronica realized that she was able to cover 75 percent of the page content, while Jeremy could barely remember anything he had read.

When asked how it went, Veronica said:

"I find myself reading through the lines and it was so vivid to me, I could grasp the content at once without necessarily giving much thought. It's pretty much the same studying experience I have all the time...that's the way I study."

Jeremy said:

"I don't know to explain, it was a Greek to me. I usually don't do so well under pressure and I guess that was what happened. While I was supposed to be reading, I was there wondering why I agreed to put myself under so much intense pressure when I know how badly I do under pressure. I know myself pretty well, and normally, I usually start studying for the semester at the beginning of the semester...that's how I get my A's unapologetically. Veronica is a genius, she needs pressure to study. It's like she is most effective when she's under pressure. And I guess that's the point of being different. We are both A students but we get our A's using totally different approaches."

With no further questioning, we can see that Veronica and Jeremy are two straight-A students who have different study approaches. Veronica apparently grasps very fast while Jeremy has to take it all in bit by bit. This doesn't mean that Veronica is smarter or more intelligent than Jeremy; after all, they both get their A's. This is to validate the fact that we are different beings and we have different functionalities; which we can effectively manage our memories.

So who then is a fast reader and who is a slow reader?

In all sincerity, we can basically just say a fast reader is Veronica Baines, while a slow reader is Jeremy Knowles, but that would only nullify the credibility of the subject because we have to be as subjective as we can be. A fast reader is one who finds it rather easy to grasp study preoccupations within a short frame of time. A slow reader is one who has to systematically and gradually take in a study preoccupation over an extended period for the sake of effective study.

It would be deceptive on your path to think that being a fast reader is a plus or to say being a slow reader is a minus. In this equation, there is no plus or minus; you simply just act out what your functionality permits you and strategically utilize it for your betterment.

## DO YOU HAVE POWER BEHIND YOUR FOCUS?

Have you found that thing yet? That very thing that keeps you focused when you are trying to fit in the sewing thread into the sewing needle, just like the seamstress from Downtown Abbey. It doesn't necessarily have to be something so deep or abstract, it doesn't have to be something the world will stand in wonder of, and it definitely doesn't have to be something you particularly love so much. What's the point here? The point is that a desire is enough for you.

"A desire is enough to be the power behind your focus."

At a first glance, when you see how tiny the needle hole is, it is enough to discourage your goal to insert anything into it. In fact, it could pass for one of those dreams that can seem pathetically unrealistic to achieve at a first look. But judging by the seamstress' remarks, there was something that kept her going even when she faced the same challenge every day she had to work; and it was the assurance that fitting the thread into the needle can actually work. She had done it all her life and she was sure it would work even if she missed it a couple of times. As a student, what is that thing that drives you? Are you driven by the fear of failing or the assurance of succeeding? Actually whatever you feed off determines what you get out of it.

Don't get it all wrong, this is still a question being painted right at your face – this is not some motivational narrative. At this point, an honest evaluation of yourself is what you need. You are indeed in school, you are indeed studying what you love – and if not, you are studying what you have to study just to get whatever it is you have to get out of it, it is true you want to excel at whatever it is your discipline is, and it is true you want a better result out of your examinations. The question is: Why do you want a better result? Do you have a reason for that?

The amazing thing is that your reason can be as simple as just wanting to graduate with the best grade, proving your parents and relatives wrong, becoming a motivation to your kids, being able to secure a good job, or for self-appraisal. Whatever the reason is, just know that there is no bad reason – the most important thing is for you to have a reason to want something better. And that reason will stand as the power behind your focus whenever the thread doesn't fit into the needle.

Do you also think your memory is very poor or can't possibly make something good out of it? You have seen the capacity of your memory earlier and you've certified that there is no bad memory. Believe this, knowing the capacity of your memory is enough to power for your focus. Knowing you used to think everything was bigger than your memory – now that you know for sure that nothing is bigger than your memory, it is enough to motivate you to stay focused even when it doesn't make sense to you.

So, the question remains the question: Do you have power behind your focus?

If not, find it! It is within you! But you won't find it until you seek it – so, find it!

## DO YOU KNOW YOUR TIME?

There is absolutely nothing as liberating as knowing when to do something and when not to do something. Narrowing it down to a student's life, there is absolutely nothing as liberating as knowing what time of the day works for your effective study experience. Some people study best at night while some study best during the day. And for all of history, there haven't yet been any scientific or biological claims that say studying best at night is better than studying best during the day. Of course, there have been recommendations that express bodily functions at various hours of the day and how to leverage on them, but we can't say for sure that one is better than the other – it entirely depends on how you've trained your study muscle.

It is essentially necessary for you to know your time – otherwise put, you have to know the time of the day you feel more relaxed – which will give you a high chance of assimilating better. Knowing your time also has to do with your study duration.

A couple of students were asked how long they sit to study. They all had different time ranges – but two amongst them gave surprising responses.

"I'm not sure I can ever feel fulfilled if I study less than 8 hours whenever I sit to study. That has been my culture since freshman year and I don't see anything changing that". Said the first student.

"It's quite different for me – I basically just take it in

bit by bit. I'm not a very stable person. I like being active, that's how I feel like an actual human. I can't recall having sat down for more than one hour in a spot studying – never. And if anyone says I have, I probably wasn't the one the person saw. I can't do anything more than an hour even if I tried. I'd literally feel like a farm animal – chained and controlled...And I don't want to ever feel that way...no, I wasn't wired for such. This is how I do it, I sit and study for about an hour, go get some sandwich or burger – depends on how I feel, come back and study for about an hour, then watch an episode of "You" on Netflix, and get back to studying for about an hour – then I'm done for the day". Said the second student.

The question is: Do you know your time?

# Chapter Five

# THE PLACE OF FOCUS AND PREPARING THE MEMORY

The human memory is the protagonist of our actions. That is to say, the mind drives our actions. It is an engine house. However, this engine works in such a way that it only reproduces what is put in. The memory is quite unlimited. It can absorb and process a lot of information however, you will have to train the memory and put in some effort to facilitate the powers it has. There is a lot of effort required from every individual to take the operations of their memory from the realm of mere perception of ideas to the realm of concrete conceptualization of those ideas or stimuli to produce required information and responses.

For students, you might have wondered why you sometimes find it difficult to fully represent information in a convincing, precise and satisfying manner despite the effort you put in gathering this information. You might have spent some minutes scribbling down points from different parts of a text or might have spent some hours listening to some recorded speeches but might not totally grasp the full concept of the data in a way that you can fully represent. One big question that many students or people generally have been asking and will probably continue to ask is; is it my study pattern? Sometimes, we may try to develop a reading pattern or reading strategy. I think quite a number of us attempted using reading time tables back in high school. That was a very industrious approach to studying which worked well for some and not so well for some others.

Also, with working-class people, it is possible that with all the hustle and bustle of everyday requirements, we let slip of some information. Perhaps, we might be too tired to sit behind the computer trying to put some information about an upcoming presentation in our heads. It is not that we are lazy. It is just that we might just have got our fingers in many pies. Now, we must appreciate that human memory can store a myriad of information. It is probably not a new thing for us to be intimated with the fact that our memory is unlimited. However, we might just be drawn to ask why sometimes it seems we cannot access some "files" when we need them. Sometimes, it looks like there is a block, a barrier that has to be removed for us to access some spaces in the memory.

Therefore, the situation might require us to ask another important question; how was the information stored? Some of us might have sat for exams and come upon a question and we feel like "I have seen this before" but ultimately struggle to conjure the right response. Again, we might have been in situations where we go "I have heard that before" but we might not be able to fully relay the information. The problem might be one of how we say or hear the data and how the memory conceptualized it. There is a pathway between perception (empirical experience) of the environment or stimulus through the senses and conceptualization of this information in the memory; the focus is the key facilitator of this pathway. The focus is purpose-driven. You have the responsibility of attaching an aim to every action. There is a result you want to get but there are ways of getting to that result.

One of the mistakes we tend to make in our activities is that we want to achieve far too many in one take. It is great to want to get to do things faster and simpler but sometimes we compromise on process. The way the human brain works, it is very fast. Messages are sent from the sense organs which are like the input devices of the system. Messages sent are interpreted in ultra-split seconds and this information is relayed inappropriate actions. However, it is different working when it comes to mastering, understanding and conceptualizing concepts that have to do with human reasoning, relationship, and innovations and that is why sometimes, you might want to quickly write someone off as dull.

## AIMS, GOALS, AND OBJECTIVES; THE VEHICLES OF FOCUS

We must embrace the understanding that every action drives at an aim. A business has an aim. That aim encapsulates the purpose for which it has been established. However, that is just the bigger ground; you need to manage the space and make this simpler and more defined. Thus, we then have goals that are tailored towards that bigger aim. They are the specific results that would define the achievement of the aim. Then, there are objectives which are the action plans, the specific course of actions, arrangements or setups that will facilitate the achievement of goals. This is also very relevant to the way we train our memory. The human memory can store any information. We have also tried to say that how this information is stored is also important thus, we have to underline the aim, goals, and objectives of our studies, plans, and activities to generate the focus that we need to facilitate effective assimilation.

Students and young adults particularly would find this a little fascinating. Are you saying we have to break down every action into aims, goals, and objectives? Maybe not all, but pretty much. The thing is actions have to be measurable. It is easy to say I want to understand something perhaps a subject, a person, a car, a movie and so on. The next question is how do you understand it? How do you show that understanding? It thus requires you to bring your focus to actionable goals and objectives. The power of focus is such that when you have something to run at, you give it all it takes. It is easier to focus on the parts and bring every part together to form a whole. The mistake perhaps is that sometimes, we are busing ourselves trying to swallow a whole without breaking it into parts.

## GENERATING FOCUS

It does not matter what anybody does. Nobody can make you give a hundred percent to any course if there is no motivation. Also, to create that motivation, there must be a goal, a vision or an ambition that you want to get. These will help you generate the kind of focus that pushes you to take decisive actions that move you towards that goal. Every other thing that leads you away from the goal is a distraction that you do not need.

You need to be as economical as possible with your time. Time is everything and it is the most precious commodity. People say there is no time. In hindsight that can be true but at the same time, the issue is more of if the action is worth your time in the first place. The way the human memory works, we keep perceiving new things every second because we are in conscious contact with our environment but then we can only spend time actively thinking or working on one concept at a time. I cannot say I want to study for a test and go to the movies at the same time. I have to look to my goal and ambition and then weigh which action helps me achieve that goal and then I give myself to that. The thing about focus is that it is time demanding. As much as footballers, for example, are doing a job we feel is so cool, they do not have as much fun as we do because they know they need to manage their time and participate in activities that will keep them fit both physically and mentally.

Furthermore, we must note that in managing our time, planning is of utmost importance. One of the characteristics of goals is that they are time-bound. The time frame is not to put you under pressure. Rather, it is to help you coordinate your actions in related activities that help you get to your goals in a faster, more effective and more efficient way. Planning just like in business helps you look ahead and prepare for the upcoming events. Some of us struggle to maintain focus because we lack plans. And when we talk about plans now, we are talking about measurable outcomes or activities. For example, a student to learn algebra will have plans like buying materials such as textbooks or handouts on the concept and then spending quality time-solving questions, seeking explanations and so on. It is easier to manage your time and coordinate your focus when you have structured plans.

Also, you want to take rest, exercise and sleep more seriously. People tend to forget that they are human beings and that nature can simply not be cheated. You see students taking coffee and trying to stay up late to study for a test. It does not work that way because your brain needs rest and sleep is one of the most important tools for information processing by the brain. Also, you come with revitalized focus after having a good rest. Exercises are also very important as you stretch your mind too.

Apart from the above-listed points that have already been made there are also a few ways that you can also generate focus in your daily activities. I might seem tricky but be rest assured practicing the following will give you an edge in being focused.

## 1. PREPARE YOUR BRAIN

The core of fulfilling any task is preparation and it is almost impossible to do anything right if your brain isn't prepared for it, most especially if it is a task that takes time or a great amount of energy. You'll need to able to take a couple of minutes to prepare yourself. Let your brain know this is what you want to do. Don't just jump into it.

## 2. SETTING PRIORITIES (UNDERSTAND WHERE YOUR FOCUS NEEDS TO BE)

First of all, we need a vivid or clear picture of what we want to achieve. A student that wants to finish with a good grade from college would be driven by the vivid picture of himself receiving the prize for the best student award. There must be a deep level of thought as to what we want to achieve. Serious-minded people don't just go about life anyhow. They have a clear vision so every action they are taking is geared towards that clear vision. It is like the architectural design of the house you wish to build. The building would be in accordance with the provisions of the drawings.

Just imagine holding a prominent post in a reputable company, or being a political leader of the country and you can't even your priorities right. You, of course, need to know where your focus needs to be because if what you're doing is worth doing at all then it demands 100% of you. If not the whole 100% percent, I understand sometimes you need to balance the scale between a lot of things most especially if the job you do demands multitasking, it might not be as easy to give 100% compared to someone who is just doing one thing. Therefore, if at all you can't give it 100% give it enough for you to be able to fulfill it on time and done with professionalism and perfection.

## 3. USE THE INTERNET INTENTIONALLY

This part is more crucial to social network freaks that can't seem to get off the internet of just a minute. Of course, the world is advancing, and it is almost impossible to not use the internet. As a matter of fact, most of our lives is controlled by information and the internet is the information bank. The point of being focused is to give no room for distraction. In order to achieve this in the realities of our world, you will have to be parsimonious and intentional when using the internet to study. Is there a way you can cut down on distractions with social media for those of us using our phones? Do you have an app freezer? Can you get yourself to give total concentration to your research? I think this also goes with a lot of discipline and frugality.

## 4. DRINK SOME COFFEE

There are of course pros and cons when it comes to doing anything at all but the key word is always the same- discipline. Coffee has its neurological advantage according to studies; the caffeine helps your concentration levels. This could explain why corporate officers indulge in a cup or two. However, students tend to conclude that it helps them not to sleep off when crash reading for examinations. And of course, there are those who leverage on the caffeine for other salacious purposes. Nevertheless, a cup or two handy could aid your alertness and help you shut out distractions. Coffee does not do anything to learning ability. It only keeps you alert.

## 5. CHECK THE THERMOSTAT

This is an important factor in generating focus. One way or the other temperature can also influence our focus both positively and negatively. Of the temperature is too hot or cool in your work environment you might need to adjust the thermostat. You need to work in an environment where you will not need a fan or a sweater. Studies have shown that workers are most productive and make fewer errors in an environment that is somewhere between 68 and 77 degrees.

## 6. TURN ON SOME MUSIC

Whichever music you decide to listen to so as to be focused is definitely up to you. But of course, listening to music is very helpful because too much background noise can be very distracting. A researcher once said, "Given that musical preferences are uniquely individualized phenomena and that music can vary in acoustic complexity and the presence or absence of lyrics, the consistency of our results was unexpected." Whether it's Jazz, Soul or country music, as long as you're focused, you're good to go.

## 7. REST WHEN DUE

If working for 5 hours is the maximum you can go in a stretch, but because of the deadlines and all sorts of events, you worked longer than you're supposed to you might still need to go back to the thing you did after reaching your limit. Overloading or overworking the brain isn't good, the body needs rest. Most importantly the brain needs it as much as the body does, therefore rest when due. It's important for rechanneling focus and determination.

## 8. DOODLING

Doodling simply helps to stabilize arousal at an optimal level, keeping people awake or reducing the high levels of autonomic arousal often related to boredom as it aids in cognitive performance and recollection.

# Chapter Six

# STORING INFORMATION IN THE MEMORY

Storage is that more or less passive process of retaining information within the brain, whether within the sensory memory, the short term memory or the more permanent LTM (Long Term Memory). Each of those different stages of human memory functions as a kind of filter that helps to guide us through the flood of data that confronts us on a day to day, avoiding an overload of data and helping to stay us sane. The more the knowledge is repeated or used, the more likely it's to be retained in LTM (which is why, for instance, studying helps people to perform better on tests). This process of consolidation, the stabilizing of an engram after its initial acquisition, is treated during additional detail in a separate section.

It's become clear that long-term memories aren't stored in just one a segment of the brain, but are cosmopolitan throughout the cortex. Long-term memories are stored throughout the brain as groups of neurons that are primed to fireside together within an equivalent pattern that created the primary experience, and each component of memory is stored within the brain area that initiated it (e.g. groups of neurons within the visual cortex store a sight, neurons within the amygdala store the associated emotion, etc.). Indeed, it seems that they will even be encoded redundantly, several times, in various parts of the cortex, so that, if one engram (or memory trace) is tired, there are duplicates, or alternative pathways, elsewhere, through which the memory should be retrieved.

Therefore, contrary to the favored notion, memories aren't stored in our brains like books on library shelves but must be actively reconstructed from elements scattered throughout various areas of the brain by the encoding process. Memory storage is, therefore, an ongoing process of reclassification resulting from continuous changes in our neural pathways, and multiprocessing of knowledge in our brains.

## ROLE OF PERCEPTION AND IMAGING

Mental imagery also sometimes called "visualizing," "seeing within the imagination," "hearing within the head," "imagining the texture of," etc.) is quasi-perceptual experience; it resembles perception but occurs within the absence of the acceptable external stimuli. It is also generally understood in touch intentionality (i.e., mental images are always images of something or other), and thereby to function as a sort of representation. Visual imagination was thought to be caused by the presence of picture-like representations (mental images) within the mind, soul, or brain, but this is often not universally accepted.

Imagery experiences are understood by their subjects as echoes, copies, or reconstructions of actual perceptual experiences from their past; at other times they'll seem to anticipate possible, often desired or feared, future experiences.

One major thing that distinguishes humans from other living creatures is the way we interact with our environment. There are a structured methodology and system in place that helps us manage information and respond accordingly as we interact and come in contact with concepts and elements of our environment. When it comes to storing and coordinating information in human memory, the role of perception is very vital.

It is easy to look at perception from different angles. In customer relationship, for example, there is something called customer perception. This refers to the opinion a customer has concerning business as a result of the experiences they have had with the said business. So you see people insist on buying a particular product or dining in a particular restaurant because of the experience they have got. Now, sometimes we may have expectations of a business or a person for example and we might end up getting disappointed when we experience them firsthand. That is also a perception that is key to how we view the person or business from then on hence the saying the first impression counts.

Have you ever stopped to wonder why sometimes people have different perceptions of the same concept? One answer that psychologists will readily give is the "principle of individual differences". Actually, there are a lot of possible explanations that could be given for this however, how about we question how the information of a particular concept was presented and stored? A child who watched a person get his hand burned and a child whose hand was burned will definitely not appreciate fire the same way. The perception of one child would surely be different from the other although they will both come to the compromise that fire is not to be toyed with.

## PERCEPTION AND MEMORY

Perception is fundamental for learning to take place. You need to come in contact with and experience the stimulus or data which will be processed and registered. Perception, learning and human memory are interrelated. It is an integrated process that is driven and coordinated by neural activities in the brain. It is a neurological process.

If we are considering human perception through the

sense organs which serve as the gateways into the brain, we will appreciate that seeing, hearing, tasting, feeling and smelling are key modes of getting information into the memory. We know the taste of some foods because we have tasted them before. As a matter of fact, if we have seen the food prepared before us, we can, after a couple of observations, go ahead and prepare the same dish yourself as many times. All these are possible because of the messages being transmitted as a result of neurological activities. The underlying factor here is experience.

## PROCESS OF MEMORY STORAGE AND RETRIEVAL

Already we can establish from several studies that perception, learning, and memory are interconnected. Let us think about the human memory process as a computer system. There is an input system made up of devices through which data is fed into the computer system for processing. Then, there is a processing unit where all the associations and interpretations are coordinated and the data is processed to bring about the information that is subsequently moved to the storage unit for easy identification and retrieval on demand through the output unit. It is a very long process that takes place in split seconds. The activities of different neurons are responsible but we are not here for plenty of science talk.

## CONCEPTUALIZING THE HUMAN MEMORY

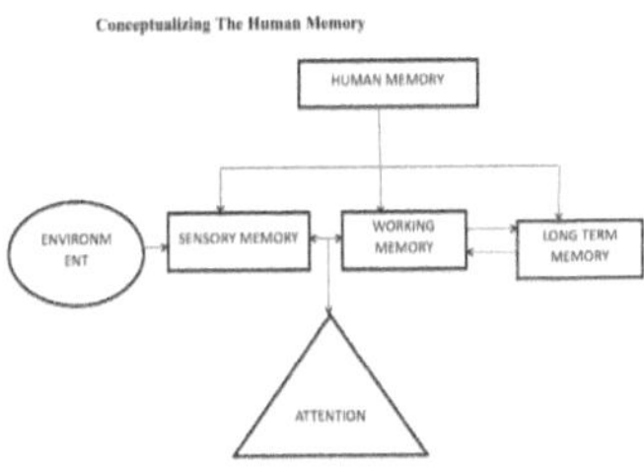


The diagram above will help us in our further discussions. Now, in trying to understand how we create memories or better yet, how we can store and process information, it is important to also consider that the relationship between the sensory memory and the environment is vital hence, our attempt to discuss perception. As a result of our contact with different information or stimuli in the environment such as that individual you come across or those texts you have to read up ahead of a presentation or those business clauses you are thinking of effecting, our memory is ignited into action which could give us a form of hysteria or illusion that we know what we are about. Yet the process has to be completed. That means we need to consciously translocate these experiences into the long term memory where they can be accessed on-demand just like the computer system.

Now the human memory from the above image has been subdivided into three parts. The sensory memory essentially selects information from the environment through the activities of the sense organs and the nerves. We are talking about the five sense organs which encapsulate visual, auditory, tactile, gustatory and olfactory activities (eyes, ear, skin, tongue, and nose). The information retrieved by the sensory memory does not last long at all. In most cases, it takes roughly 0.5 seconds for visual information to last in this memory (sensory) for audio messages you still have the grace of 3-4 seconds to enjoy the waves. The reason for the speed or volatile nature of the sensory memory is simply because it is involved in perception and humans are constantly adapting to the changing environment which means they constantly come upon new data and information that need to be translated. It never stops and thus, there is always a new thought, feeling, impression, knowledge and so on that all have to be interpreted.

Then, we have a working memory. A working memory is like an active memory. It just like a case of having different assignments from school or work and you select the one that you want to work on. The working memory requires a very high level of attention and focus on details. You can say this is where you are actively involved in the process of arranging and conceptualizing the information in such a way that can be easily retrieved and reproduced when stored in the long term memory. The working memory comprises of what you are thinking about at any given instance. For example, you have seen some figures in your math quiz and you are beginning to attempt to understand the concept and how the workings led you to arrive at the given figures. It requires active attention.

One of the beautiful findings of psychologists and neurologists is that the working memory holds more information than the sensory memory but you can only be working on a few related concepts at a time. The major thing to note here is you are engaging in some repetitive actions to aid the conceptualization of the information you are getting. Focus is important as you cannot be multitasking on unrelated activities. Working memory refers to the ability to maintain and use and reflect over the information in a short period despite factors of distraction also taking place around the information. A lot of scholars have posited that the working memory capacity is of central importance in a wide range of higher-order cognitive functions, such as reasoning, problem-solving, and language comprehension. Recently, interest in the enhancement of working memory capacity has increased as a result of the success and popularity of working memory-training.

Lastly, the long term memory is simply the memory bank. When we are talking about the potential of the memory and how you can access a myriad of information and take actions based on certain experiences, this is the area of the memory we are talking about.

However, you will only succeed in turning that potential into a reality when you can successfully transpose information into the long term memory which is the goal of the majority of our activities and experiences as humans. There are cases of students for example that go into the examination halls having spent quite a few hours reading and maybe get stocked in on a question that looks so familiar. They might be able to remember themselves looking at the question but would be distressed that they cannot seem to adequately recall the information. The point is, they have not completed the storage process perhaps. We must, however, bear in mind that memories are not entirely the perfect replica of the real world. However, whatever gets stored in the long term memory is relatively permanent.

One key thing to take note of is that whereas the human brain has the unlimited capacity to store information, there will be relative lag if this information is not retrieved regularly. Also, one must be drawn to the relationship between emotional intensity attached to experiences and the storage and retrieval of such information. I think one easy way to liken this is by considering the concept of the scale of preference. The most important things come first. Well, in the case of human memory, the information is prioritized by how much emotional reaction we have towards a particular action. So it holds that things we have a stronger emotional reaction to are very much likely to be more important than those we scarcely notice. We most definitely would have been in situations where someone tries to remind us of something they are convinced we have done or we were part of but we might not be able to recall. Sometimes we could simply ask "are you sure that happened"? And they are like "were you not there"? Sometimes it is not that you had a blackout or you are suffering from any degree of amnesia. The issue here is that you did not pay attention and thus you were not able to generate any form of emotional reaction to what happened.

Going back to the concept of sensory memory, perception and the key role of attention, we can consider that after so many years, some people can recreate how they felt about something they experienced some time ago. We could argue a case for a relationship between emotional attachment and memory as a result of attention. For example, when going through an autobiography, you would notice the attention to detail and how the writer delves deeply to recreate some key and critical points in his life or career. In most cases, they can recreate these life events in such a way that you feel like you are in their shoes and you can feel what they felt. That is the power of attention and memory. Now there could be some other events that do not create as much spark, not that they did not experience it but the emotional reaction to those events was not as intense because probably they did not muster enough attention there.

## THE PRIMARY ROLE OF ATTENTION AND INFORMATION STORAGE

The importance of attention cannot be overemphasized. Already we talked about focus and how you try to narrow down your coverage to one particular thing at a time. Also, we have seen from the above, the sensory memory which basically conducts perception does not hold much for too long because we are constantly adapting to the changing environment and thus we are constantly experiencing new things, new impulses, and sensations as a result of the various stimuli we are getting. Thus, the major factor that gets us ruminating on specific information in our working memory is attention.

Attention is such a pervasive and perhaps vague concept to try to conceptualize. A lot of psychologists have in the past tried to put a definition on the term. The major underlying idea holds that the brain has to select between the information of importance and those of not much importance. One explanation that has been put forward as a fundamental factor for attention is the availability of resources (content, objects, ideas, places, people ....). Attention is resource-demanding but the working memory can only attend to a limited number of resources at a time for adequate concentration. Yes, I know sometimes we have been challenged to be multitasking but with the memory as powerful as it is, there are only a few tasks you can attend to and generate the adequate emotional reaction to at a time which will help your brain with its selection for which experience to store in the long term or which one gets written off after some time.

Learning anything from language to mathematical formulae or chemical compounds or even the likes or dislikes of a partner or friend depends on three critical processes which are; attention, encoding, and retrieval. The key concept here is that any information you cannot retrieve easily and regularly has not been learned.

Now, attention is the first and most important process in the sense that you will need to attach some level of focus and concentration to the material, object or person. We are going to look at this practically. A teacher is taking a language class of just five students. Three of them are really focusing their attention on what the teacher is saying. They are taking note of the sound pronunciation and the way he constructs the sentences. The other two are also looking at the teacher but are not really into what is going on. The teacher gives a short quiz at the end of the class and the other two students were not in the top three. Now the primary reason is perhaps they were not paying enough attention. We need attention to deal with and sort through a huge amount of sensory information. That is, as our mind gets fed with new information perpetually, we have to give priority to new information to generate the appropriate emotional response.

Of course, there are key principles of human development and the principle of individual uniqueness is such a unique one. It holds conversely that different people are going to assimilate information in different ways at a different pace. However, at the root of it is the input of attention.

## LEARNING FASTER WITH THE MEMORY

The goal of learning anything is to be able to reproduce it when required. There needs to be an observable change in behavior or learning has not taken place. The end game for us is to try to get information into the long term memory because that is where the information needs to be stored for easier retrieval when required. Commitment to lifelong learning is one of the basic ingredients for wholesale success for anything in life and in dealing with human memory, it is very important to be determined to learn new things. Whatever the memory does not use regularly dies off easily.

There are four basic tips or shall we say secrets to enhancing faster learning and retention of anything at all with the human memory; learn, reflect, implement and; share. These four secrets can be grouped into two; input and output. The major trick for us here is that we must try to focus more on output than input. One thing that is quite ironic is that we think we learn better or achieve more by studying more and more materials. Learning is important and to facilitate that, you need to focus and pay rapt attention. One of the inhibitors of learning is multitasking. The working memory can only deal with a couple of things at a time and if you are going to learn adequately, you need to do away with distractions. You need to get yourself into the activity and be as active and participatory as possible.

Then you must reflect on the information garnered. Here, you are asking questions. You are trying to analyze the information and map out the relationship between different aspects of the data. you are going to the next level of attempting to draw your conclusions on different concepts based on the data or information presented.

Next, you implement it. The information you have gotten is of no good if you do not put them to the good news by carrying out specific actions. The statement practice makes perfect is not just for literary effect. Whatever you do not do, you do not learn. That is why practice is really needed. A football player can watch YouTube videos showing many football skills but will not be able to reproduce any of them if he does not practice. This is also why educationist insists on a lot of classroom activity. The truth is the best way to master something is by learning through practice. You do not forget to ride a bicycle because you spent time riding it so the principle remains with you. So if you are learning a language, for example, you will do better by attempting to use the words you pick up more often.

Lastly, you have to share what you have learned. One thing people tend not to realize in the world of learning is that the more you share, the more you gain. Sharing helps you acquire more knowledge and rub minds with other people; which ultimately opens you up to better angles on the information.

# Chapter Seven

# LEARNING LANGUAGES IN A SHORT TIME

Have you ever paused to think of what really made the world so fond of singer/dancer Shakira? According to one of the many articles that have chronicled her artistic genius; she was tagged as one of the female leaders of pop culture. Her artistic prowess has indeed proven to be one of the very best. Back to what made the world so fond of her; it wasn't necessarily her musical skill or dance flexibility; it was a function of the fact that she could sing so well, dance so effortlessly and speak Portuguese, English, and Italian very fluently.

You have probably never thought of her language dexterity – what do you care anyway? All you want is to be entertained right? Aside from Shakira, there are hosts of other Hollywood celebrities who are known to be multi-lingual and their abilities to speak different languages have proven to be one of the benchmarks of their career. It is quite obvious that people are particularly fascinated by individuals who can speak a language that is not a language they are familiar with.

This reality will always bring to remembrance the story of two lovebirds who fell in love solely on the grounds of being able to speak various languages. Anytime they met to hang out, they'd teach themselves new vocabulary and a lot of other things to be known about a particular language. By virtue of this, their bond was strengthened and their chemistry grew even deeper than they ever thought it'd grow. They didn't have to force communication even when they had nothing to talk about; by default, they knew when they ran out of things to say, they could just decide to silence the cluelessness by sharpening each other's language skill. They were really adorable and they became the cynosure of all eyes. Everyone wanted to be like them. Everyone wanted to be able to speak other languages as if being able to speak other languages was a passport to wealth. Well, in the reality of pop culture, being multilingual can actually be a passport to wealth for many.

Yet again, this is not a love story, neither is this a storybook. All these twists, metaphors and stories are just to relax your mind and make you see things clearly. The fact being laid here is that there is so much you can do with yourself and it solely lies on how effectively you maximize the power of your memory.

Have you always wanted to be able to speak different languages? Have you tried learning a language and you had to stop after a couple of classes because you weren't just getting it or you felt your memory couldn't handle it?

Here is how to do it...

## HOW TO FINALLY LEARN THAT LANGUAGE

### Be Focused

Knowing how to finally learn that language doesn't erase where we started from – which is The Power of Focus.

So what exactly is the power behind your focus? Otherwise, put, why exactly do you feel the need to learn a new language? Know this for sure, there is no reason too weak to want to learn a language. You don't have to go as deep as telling yourself you want to learn a new language because you want to become a diplomat and bridge the gap between quarreling nations and all of that – no, not everyone has that dream. The point is that – as much as everyone should dream big, you really don't need a big reason to learn a language before you learn it. Your reason could be as simple as just learning so you could be able to interact with your friends from other nations, or just learning it so you can fulfill another list on your must-dos. So there is absolutely no reason to simple for you to learn a new language; all that matters is for you to have a reason which you already do.

Whatever your reason for learning a new language is; let it be the power behind your focus. Even when it gets tough and it seems like your memory cannot handle it, let your reason push you even further. Let it encourage you when nothing does. The truth is that, whenever your brain or anyone tells you there's no way you can learn that language, it is a lie. We have established the fact that your brain can take unlimited information. So it is very possible to acquire that new language you've always wanted to acquire.

And if nothing pushes you when you feel discouraged, always remember that your memory is enough to accommodate whatever appears to be bigger than it. All you need to do is to keep at it and never give up.


## WHAT YOU NEED TO KNOW BEFORE LEARNING THE LANGUAGE

Do you know that what you are trying to do is called Second Language Acquisition? This means that coupled with your first language which you have been able to acquire naturally from birth, you are seeking out to acquire a language that is totally different from what you are used to. And in all sincerity, second language acquisition comes with a lot of difficulties at the beginning but the good news is that there is nothing too difficult for your memory to accommodate.

The way you developed your first language is

completely different from the way you will develop your second language. Your first language naturally grew on you as a result of your upbringing and exposure. You naturally picked the tongue you were used to and developed a language culture from there over time. Now that you are willing to learn another language, you can't go through the natural process of acquiring a first language. If so, you'd have to perhaps go back to being an infancy toddler. Acquiring a new language will take you through the formal learning of the language – which means you'll have to sign up for a language class or probably get a tutor to put you through it.

The challenge of learning a new language isn't particularly in how difficult the language is, it is usually how long it'd take to learn the language. Many people don't want to go through the long-lasting process of cramming and memorizing series of language vocabularies; they just want to know as soon as they can so they can show off. Well, there are a few factors that guide the fast learning of a language.

Follow through...


## SET A LANGUAGE LEARNING GOAL

If you ask men who have been able to prove and show their greatness to the world, they will tell you they couldn't have achieved everything they achieved without goal setting. Goal setting is what shows you the way, takes you through the way, and gets you to your destination.

## What inspires your goal setting?

Your goal setting is inspired by the reason you plan to acquire a new language. If you want to learn a new language to give you an edge when applying for a high paying job, great – let that push you to set goals for yourself. When setting your goals, let them be time-bound. Make sure you write down everything you want to achieve and when you want to achieve them. Attaching a time-bound to your goals makes your goals more credible and motivating for you. It makes a lot of difference because whenever you are reminded you have set a goal to have attained a particular level of mastery, it pushes you to go harder if you've perhaps been slacking.

Do you want to learn it for 6 months, 12 months or 2 days? It doesn't matter how long you want to learn it; it all depends on whatever works for you. Just be sure that you have a timeframe for yourself and you stick with it. And whatever time you set for yourself, make sure it's very realistic. In this case, you have to be brutally honest with yourself in setting a timeframe for your second language acquisition. It is literally not something you get a hang of overnight, it is something you need consistent practice to fully grasp.

Know this – you cannot set a timeframe of 2 days

for learning Spanish to the point of the intermediate level if you have never even attempted speaking Spanish before; it's just not realistic. You need to be very real and easy on this. As much as you want to learn it really fast, you have to also be smart with your timing.

Don't just set the timeframe; let it be the power that strengthens your focus. Never stray from it. Keep at it. Your memory can accommodate it.

## CHANGE YOUR ATMOSPHERE

A funny guy once said that anytime he's being told to change his atmosphere, he regarded the statement in that he was moving out of his immediate surroundings – more like evacuating his home. But that is not what we are talking about; changing your atmosphere in this sense is totally different from moving out of your immediate surroundings or evacuating your home – what it simply means is creating an atmosphere that inspires the language you are trying to learn.

Why does this matter? Why do you have to create an atmosphere to learn a new language?

A Swedish decent once came for a job interview in a British firm. In the light of the traditional organization culture that warrants a well-meaning conversation between the employer and the employee, she got into a conversation with one of the interviewers and to the interviewer's surprise, she spoke raw British English with a profound British accent that one would have thought she had lived in Britain all her life. Interestingly, she had never traveled to England or any English speaking country until that short period she had to travel down for an interview. She was flawless with her delivery and she literally blew everyone's mind with how she was able to eloquently vocalize the English language with a deep British accent.

This sparked curiosity in the mind of the interviewer – she was then asked how she was able to master the language and accent so perfectly.

In a concentrated British accent, she said:

"I guess I basically just knew what I wanted and went for it. It was definitely not easy from the start but I kept at it. It was pretty difficult while learning because I had only my best friend to speak English with. I couldn't speak English with my family because they cared for nothing more than potato fries which I understood. I had to change my atmosphere – not move out of my house; of course, that would mean me getting ready for compulsory emancipation. I couldn't leave even if I wanted to. What really helped me was what I surrounded myself with: I started an online English class that literally felt like Greek to me at first. The worst part was the fact that the class was being facilitated by an Indian who had studied English at Oxford University. And I'm sure you know what that means – his Indian accent got in the way even though he had an in-depth knowledge of the language. After a couple of weeks, I started understanding the language but I couldn't speak it. Then I figured that I needed to surround myself with British materials and by British materials, I mean movies, interviews, conferences, music and everything that had British on it. And having a best friend who was driven by achieving the same goal made it easier. We'd meet up and speak British till we became obsessed. Our obsession led to profound mastery and that's what got me here."

Changing your atmosphere is very important and it aids fast learning. You need to surround yourself with materials that would help. If possible, live, breathe and eat the new language.

## GET YOURSELF A PARTNER IN CRIME

No, this isn't another Bonnie and Clyde episode – the world definitely doesn't need another Bonnie and Clyde. This is a metaphor for "get yourself a friend or friends you'd learn together with". Knowing that you are not alone in a learning process has a way of inspiring and motivating you to go harder even when you don't feel like it. Frankly, there are days you'd feel discouraged and want to give up on language learning goals; but when you have a support system to strengthen you, it makes all the difference. You wouldn't have to run the race alone, you'd have a partner in crime to break through your goals and beyond.

And if you are lucky – meaning if you are the luckiest person on the entire planet, you'd get yourself partners who are willing to embark on the same journey with you. You sure do know that there is power in number. Take for instance you have about five friends who are on the same language learning journey with you, learning would be swift and easy for you because you will have people to discuss what you are learning with. Every time you guys meet to discuss the language, each person will definitely have something different to teach the rest of you; this way, you are learning without necessarily making all the effort. You are basically learning through the support system you have carved out for yourself.

An English high school sophomore who never had a plan to learn Spanish once gave an account of how he learned Spanish so fast...

In his words:

"I never had the plan to; in fact, I was never fascinated by the language but somehow, it grew on me and I found myself learning it so fast rather unconsciously. I had a couple of friends during my sophomore year in high school who wanted to learn Spanish more than anything. We'd go to the court every evening to play basketball but every time we went, we ended up speaking Spanish instead of playing basketball. To date, I still can't connect the dots between Spanish and Basketball – I find it rather strange. A frustrated me would sit there and get even more frustrated as to how a group of youngies would set out to play basketball and all they ended up doing was to speak Spanish. It didn't make sense to me but there was no other person I could hang out with. I stuck around and listen to everything they say to each other. They'd say a couple of phrases and clauses in Spanish and translate them into English. So unconsciously, Spanish began to sink in till I could speak like them. They were very surprised when they realized I could speak everything they could speak. I had no formal education in Spanish learning, I basically just sat with a couple of friends who were learning Spanish and it grew on me."

## START WITH THE BASICS

Would it not seem quite overwhelming and discouraging if a person set out to learn the English Language and the first thing the person is trying to learn is how to say – "we are not a product of an astronomical random chance." It definitely won't cut it – it's definitely too complicated for a fresh learner of the language.

When learning a new language, it is always better to start by learning the common greeting words of the language. Words like:

- Good morning
- How do you do?
- What is your name?
- Can I help you?
- Where do you live?
- How was your day?

- Are you well?
- Where do you live?
- How much is this?

And so on...

Starting with the basics draws you into the language and gives you a sense of identifying with the language when all you still know is the basics. When you take it gradually, it helps your memory accommodate it faster. You should treat the language the same way you'd treat an infancy toddler. You cannot start feeding an infancy toddler with tough barbeque meat at his/her infancy stage; that would mean you are trying to kill the toddler before time. You have to start by introducing soft food like milk, water, soft cereals, etc. So, don't try to kill your memory before time; take it gradually and build it from there. Make sure you take it one step at a time.

One of the many mistakes people who set the goal of learning a new language is trying to learn fast so they can impress people. Don't get trapped in the idea of trying to impress people with your German or whatever language you choose to learn – that time will come when you would not have to impress anyone, by merely speaking it, people would be impressed and perhaps even come to you to teach them. If you set your mind on trying to impress people with the new language, you just might never understand what you need to understand. There just might never be a strong foundation for what you are trying to learn. Calm yourself down and take it to step by step. You indeed want to learn it really fast – but there is something greater than just learning fast, and it is learning well and learning good.

So when you start with learning the language, make sure you start from the basics. And make sure you practice the basics really well. Actually, the complexities of all languages ride on the strength of their basics. So most complex words in every language, still have their root words featuring in every speech act.

To get the full picture, try imagining the Empire State building without a foundation to hold it together – that would be the greatest tragedy there is. So, learning a language needs a very strong foundation as the Empire State building.

## DON'T BE AFRAID OF MAKING MISTAKES

"In an article I wrote for a lifestyle magazine, I expressed my thoughts on being afraid of making mistakes so profoundly. After the magazine got published, I got a lot of emails from readers telling me how much my article had blessed them. I felt so great about it because it made me feel like I was actually living for something for the very first time. I was a victim of the fear of making mistakes for a huge part of my life. The fear of making mistakes was so profuse in me that I could barely do anything without making a mistake. Even conversations felt like a herculean task because no matter how hard I tried, mistakes were bound to happen. This fear went ahead to cripple my self-esteem until I could not even see myself anymore. I literally became a grasshopper because I thought I couldn't do anything right. Well, I was actually not doing anything right back then; I was making a lot of mistakes, and I'm sure my mistakes were so proud of me because they knew even if I couldn't make anything, I'd make them. I'm sure it made them feel really good.

The moment I was liberated from my fear of mistakes was the moment I realized that mistakes are signs of progress – meaning if your life is devoid of mistakes then you are probably not living at all. That period was the period I was studying Chinese as an English student. It was a pretty significant moment in my life because my mastery of the Chinese language would determine my promotion. I knew I shouldn't tank it. I knew I shouldn't fail at learning it. I shouldn't even accommodate the thoughts of failing Chinese. But the more I tried not to, the more the thoughts kept rushing into my memory like a tidal wave, opposing every positive vibe inside of me.

Summarizing my long story, I failed at it a lot of times, about ten times. And I wasn't failing because learning Chinese was bigger than my memory; I was failing because of my overwhelming fear of failing. I soon realized that the fact that I was making a lot of mistakes was an attestation that I was trying, and that was what saved me. I realized that if I wasn't trying, then I wouldn't be making a mistake, and to me, trying is a sign of progress.

So what did I do?

I simply shook the fear off, bought myself some cheeseburger kept trying, but this time around without fear and that was the moment every took shape for me – I started assimilating properly and that is why I can speak Chinese so fluently as I am right now," said Jonathan Burrows, a British investment banker who is also a writer.

Actually, while he was giving this testimony, he said it all in Chinese but it had to be translated to a language you can read since it's not everyone who can read Chinese.

Speaking of not being afraid of making mistakes while learning a new language, you should be very prepared for making mistakes. If you are thinking the ride is going to be very smooth and you are not going to make mistakes at all, then you should probably not even set the goal of learning a new language. In the real sense, learning a new language can be likened to a toddler trying to stand on his feet and walk – the toddler wouldn't definitely just start walking. He is going to start by crawling before graduating to actually walking. And even after graduating to walking, the toddler is definitely going to fall a lot of times before he masters the art of walking stamina.

Learning how to walk for a toddler is exactly the same as learning a new language – a language you were never familiar with until you decided to learn it for reasons best known to you. Know this, the fact that you make mistakes a lot of time is a sign of progress – it is a sign that you are actually learning. Mistakes don't just happen – mistakes happen because we try to do some things we believe we can do perfectly until we realize we cannot do them as perfectly as we thought we could, but the good news is that we tried it anyway.

So when you make mistakes while learning a new language, you should pat yourself on the back and be very proud of yourself for your progress. You should remember that there was a time you were not making mistakes at all – your life was totally free from mistakes and that was because you had not picked up this language challenge. Mistakes might want to discourage you, but don't let them. And frankly, the fact that you have decided to learn this language really fast makes you very prone to make mistakes as a result of learning urgencies.

Guess what, the fastest way to learn a language is to actually make mistakes and get corrected. When we make mistakes and get corrected, we learn from them and it helps us to do things right the next time – this how we grow and this is how we learn. The more mistakes you make, the faster you learn.

"The more mistakes you make, the faster you learn."

So tell your fears of mistakes to get behind you. It might be very difficult to not give in to fear most times, especially when your mistakes are so many that you begin to wonder if you have a brain at all. But the way out of this 'fear of mistake' trap is to be ready for it and get excited about it. Before you start learning the language and even while you are learning it, keep telling yourself that "mistake is a sign of progress" and "the more the mistakes I make, the faster I learn". Mistakes don't break you, they make you.

"Mistakes don't break you, they make you."

# Chapter Eight

# EFFECTIVE WAYS TO STORE MORE INFORMATION

As it has already been established that there is no limit to which you can maximize your brain; this section is to illuminate some effective techniques that will help you store more information in your memory.

It has been reported that most people find it rather difficult to remember names, numbers, and appointments most times. This is not because their memories cannot remember these things – it basically just means that they have not learned how to store more information in their brains. There is really no amount of information that his to large or enormous for your memory to capture – the question is: have you been saving this information the right way?

Are you even maximizing the full potential of your brain at all?

Here is how to store more information in your memory.

## KNOW THE LEARNING TECHNIQUE THAT WORKS FOR YOU

The fact that we are unique beings makes our learning techniques quite different from the other. The difference in learning techniques doesn't gratify one learning technique above the other learning technique – it only confirms learning doesn't have to go one way, there are a million ways with which we can learn the same thing.

For instance, have you ever wondered why the simultaneous equation in mathematics has different methods of solving it? It is so because solving a problem or learning something doesn't necessarily have to go a certain way. Just because something is popular doesn't mean it is the best way to do things.

To be able to store more information and maximize your memory, you need to understand the learning method that works for you. Some people would say they are the visual learners, some would say they are rhythmic learners, while some would say they are symbolic learners and so on. What's the difference between all these learning techniques?

A visual learner simply learns best by putting something in visual programming –which means that if they can see it play out visually; then, they can store it in their memories without ever forgetting. The rhythmic learner would prefer it in musical programming – they like to fit a piece of information in a musical piece or sound form to effectively grasp it. This is why some people prefer audiobooks to the hard copy. If they can listen to it, then they can store in their memories. And for the symbolic learners, they like in symbols. For example, when you say the word "transportation" what comes to their mind is a vehicle. They like to create a symbol for every little thing the best way that suits them. This is how they remember information. To them, if they can create a symbol for it, they can remember easily.

There is actually no best way – the best way is the one that works best specifically for you.

Find what works for you!


## TEACH IT

It has been proven that the best way to cement the information in your memory for life is to teach what you know consistently. When you store up information in your memory, teaching it helps you remember, it helps you detect what you can't remember and it also helps you discover things you never knew about the topic.

And when we say teach it, we do not mean you should go sign up for a teaching job in a school or something. In a plot to teach, you can actually teach your siblings, your parents, or even yourself by simply standing in front of your mirror recounting every piece of information you have stored. Teaching helps you recollect every detail of what you have stored and if in the process you realize there is something you are forgetting, you can just simply go back to the information source to remind yourself. Reminding yourself doesn't make you a failure or a dullard; it only means that you definitely won't forget it again the next time.

When next you store information in your memory, give yourself some time, then try teaching it; you'd realize how helpful it'd be.

## BUILD A STORY AROUND IT

Do you know that your brain loves entertainment? This is why you would easily remember the plot of a movie faster than you'd remember the information in a science textbook. This happens because the brain loves excitement. Storing up information your memory hits better if you try to fit the piece of information in a story arc so that your brain can get excited about it.

A high school freshman was asked how she remembers the nine planets – she said:

"It was difficult; I couldn't even process my thoughts every time I try to remember until I found a way out of it. That day my English teacher, Mrs. Juliana whom I love so much sat right next to Paul Wilbur, my high school crush during a varsity basketball game. I didn't know where the thought came from I just coined a story from that – "My very excellent Mrs. Juliana sits up near Paul."

It kept ringing n my head till I got home. I couldn't make sense of it at first until I remembered I had to study for my geography test the next day. I sat and tried to figure out how to store up the nine planets as always and I still couldn't figure it out. Out of frustration, I closed my textbook for a while and started writing my thoughts on a piece of paper. Then I wrote: "My very excellent Mrs. Juliana sits up near Paul." Then something told me to open my geography textbook again, and I did.

Then I realized this:

My – Mercury<br>
Very – Venus<br>
Mrs. – Mars<br>
Juliana – Jupiter<br>
Sits – Saturn<br>
Up – Uranus<br>
Near – Neptune<br>
Paul – Pluto

How amazing – did you see the excitement the story brought into her memory nerves? The excitement literally made her store up what she had been struggling to store in her memory for a long time.

# Chapter Nine

# CONCLUSION

With all that has been said, it is rather impossible to exhaust the depth of wisdom on how to maximize your memory. This is only a perspective to inspire you and let you know that nothing is too big for you to figure out. Your memory can take it all in and you are the only permission it needs to take up the challenge. If you will permit your memory by playing your part, only then would you be the master of your brain.